Brian Everitt is professor emeritus, King's College London. He retired in 2004 at the age of 60. In his career as a statistician, he wrote over 70 books on various aspects of medical and psychological statistics. Post-retirement, he now spends his time playing very gentle tennis, going on long walks and playing classical guitar in private.

Dedicated to the memory of my parents, Lucy Emily Everitt and Sidney William Everitt, and to the memory of my sisters, Joan, Hilda, Iris, Pat, Connie and Vera.

Brian Everitt

MADE IN ESSEX

Memories of an Essex Childhood

AUSTIN MACAULEY PUBLISHERS™

LONDON • CAMBRIDGE • NEW YORK • SHARJAH

All of the events in this memoir are true to the best of author's memory. The views expressed in this memoir are solely those of the author. Names of childhood friends and of a number of other people that are mentioned in the book have been changed to protect their identity. This does not apply to members of the Everitt family.

A CIP catalogue record for this title is available from the British Library.

ISBN 9781528998635 (Paperback)
ISBN 9781528998642 (ePub e-book)

www.austinmacauley.com

First Published (2021)
Austin Macauley Publishers Ltd
25 Canada Square
Canary Wharf
London
E14 5LQ

I must thank my wife, Mary-Elizabeth Everitt, for her support during the writing of this book and for her helpful suggestions on how some of the content could be improved, along with her advice about punctuation, both of which greatly improved the book.

Preface

My mother had ten children: nine girls followed by one boy, me. Three of the girls died in infancy, not particularly unusual amongst working class families in the 1930s. My youngest sister, Vera, was seven years older than me, so despite the six sisters I was surrounded by, I was, in many ways, an only child. When I was born in 1944, the family was living in Essex, and it was in Essex that I spent my childhood. No doubt, everyone thinks their childhood is, in some sense unique, and of course it is. Writing this account of my own childhood needs some explanation, in particular, to myself. Well, first is that at my age of 75, I can remember events in my childhood far easier than I can remember what book I read a few weeks ago or what my wife asked me to do today before she left for work. And related to the memory issue is that I wanted to put down accounts of events in my childhood that I remember well, some with pleasure, some with a little pain or puzzlement, before age takes its final toll and all these stories are lost to my family who have, at times, shown some vague interest in knowing more about my childhood.

Perhaps towards the end of our life, childhood memories are those we cling to the most. Like *Citizen Kane* with his 'rosebud' moment, most of us will have a childhood memory or two that recalls the happiness and innocence of that time. I certainly do.

Chapter 1

Some Background

Mum and Dad

My mum was born in 1900 and my dad five years earlier. Mum was born in Ramsgate, Kent and Dad in Norwich, Norfolk. At the age of three, Mum was sent to live in London with an aunt because the house in Ramsgate was too small to accommodate her parents, her four brothers and her. Mum then grew up in London and as a teenager got a job working as a cleaner in the London Hospital. She once told me she saw the Elephant Man, Joseph Carey Merrick there, but since he died in 1890, I think she must have seen his skeleton which was kept in the hospital. Mum's stories were, at times, prone to a little exaggeration.

Dad must have moved from Norfolk to London at some stage, probably to find work. He was enlisted into the Essex Regiment at Canning Town in 1915. His trade on enlistment was stated to be pawnbroker's assistant. Dad was sent to France to serve in the First World War. Three years later, he was invalided out of the army when he was wounded by a machine gun bullet in the inner left thigh. Dad's discharge certificate described him as 'honest, sober and reliable', and entitled to 'two wound stripes'.

Sadly, I have no idea of where my mum and dad first met, but they married in 1925 and moved into a small house in Custom House, East London. Mum stopped work at the London Hospital on her marriage. Dad worked as a labourer in the Tate and Lyle sugar factory on the Isle of Dogs.

My mum became pregnant very quickly after her marriage, and her first child, a daughter christened Joan, was born in 1926. Joan was followed with amazing regularity by eight other girls with three sadly dying in infancy. By 1937, when my youngest sister, Vera was born, the family home in Custom House had to accommodate my parents and their six daughters Joan, Hilda, Iris, Pat, Connie and Vera. The house must have been very, very cramped.

War

Two years after Vera was born, the Second World War began. In the early 1940s, London was bombed many times with the East End suffering very badly. In one particular raid, the family house in Custom House received an almost direct hit, and the Tate and Lyle factory was also set ablaze. Fortunately, none of the family was hurt. My parents and their daughters had taken refuge in an air-raid shelter with many other East Enders. When the all-clear sounded, the family returned to find a large crater containing what was left of their house and their belongings.

The family took refuge in a nearby church, and after a few days, my mum and five of her daughters were evacuated to Reading. Joan, the eldest daughter, stayed in London training to be a care home worker. Dad continued to work at what was left of the Tate and Lyle factory and stayed with friends for the time being.

The first accommodation offered to Mum in Reading was with the local vicar. This was not a success and ended with Mum making some comments asking how a man of the cloth could be so unkind to a family in need. I have no details of what led to this outburst. Luckily, the next accommodation Mum and her daughters were sent to was provided by a large house owned by an elderly couple. This couple turned out to be very kind, and they made Mum and the five daughters as comfortable as they could. After settling into the house, a school had to be found for the girls. Only a small village school was available where I think the girls were kindly treated but as they told me later in life, all they were really taught was sewing. Essentially, the War robbed them of a proper education and the possibility of a good job when the War finished.

Essex, Brentwood, Pilgrims Hatch and a Surprise

Towards the end of the War, many East Enders were eventually moved out to Harold Hill in Essex to live on a large council estate, an estate where living conditions soon became tough with a fair amount of crime, petty and otherwise. My family was more fortunate. After living in Reading for about a year or so, they all moved to a house that my dad had found to rent in a small hamlet, Pilgrims Hatch, near the town of Brentwood, several miles further East in Essex than the Harold Hill Estate. I have no idea how my dad found this house, but I know it was rented from a Mr Botting for perhaps a few shillings a week.

Essex is a county in South East England, north-east of London. It extends along the North Sea coast between the Thames and Stour estuaries. In area, it is the 11th largest of the 48 English counties, and its 350-mile-long coastline is the second longest of an English County. The name Essex has its root in the Old English name *Eastseaxe*. According to one website, Essex is 'culturally vibrant, redolent with over two thousand years of history and an economic powerhouse. Essex is a fascinating place to discover and explore.' Possibly, but as a child, my acquaintance with Essex was largely restricted to a relatively small area around where we lived, an area which included the small town of Brentwood and the even smaller hamlet of Pilgrims Hatch.

Brentwood is a town in Essex about 20 miles east-north-east of Charing Cross. The name was originally thought to derive from a corruption of the words 'burnt' and 'wood' with the name Burntwood still appearing on eighteenth-century maps of the area. But 'brent' was the Middle English for burnt. The name possibly reflects the fact that the early settlement that grew eventually into the town was part of the Forest of Essex and where the main occupation was charcoal burning. Brentwood has been an important stopping place for travellers since Roman times and was on the route that pilgrims took over the River Thames to Canterbury. A chapel dedicated to St Thomas the Martyr was built around 1221, and the ruin of the chapel remains in the high street to this day.

In his book *Tour through the Eastern Counties,* published in 1724, Daniel Defoe noted that Brentwood was a large thoroughfare town, 'full of good inns and chiefly maintained by the excessive multitude of carriers and passengers which are constantly passing this way to London with droves of cattle, provisions and manufactures'. But the town remained a relatively small hamlet until the arrival of the Eastern Counties Railway with the first trains steaming into its station in 1840.

About two miles to the North of Brentwood lies the hamlet of Pilgrims Hatch. The name is derived from twelfth-century pilgrimages to Canterbury. Pilgrims from the Midlands would pass through Pilgrims Hatch on route to Brentwood which was a popular stopping place at the time. At the time, Pilgrims Hatch was not recognised as a community as such, having only a few properties in the area which was mainly open countryside and not settled in any numbers until the twentieth century.

The house Dad had rented was in road called Broomwood Gardens, a road which ran into open fields at one end, the fields then stretching for a few hundred yards before they became the Council rubbish dump. At the other end, Broomwood Gardens was crossed by another small road leading to Ongar Road which was the main road through Pilgrims Hatch. Bordering the small back garden of the semi-detached house was a hay field. Inside the house consisted of a kitchen and two rooms downstairs; upstairs were three bedrooms, one of which was about the size of a large wardrobe. There was a bathroom which contained an ancient geyser that produced hot water for baths – sometimes! In the 1940s there was, of course, no garage on the house.

Picture 1: The house on the right is 8 Broomwood Gardens, where I was born in 1944, pictured as it is today with a garage.

In 1943 when the family moved into the house, the garden contained an Anderson air-raid shelter (named after Sir John Anderson, the man responsible for preparing Britain to withstand German air raids). The main part of the shelter was formed from corrugated steel panels and was quite cramped; a person over 6ft tall would not have been able to stand up. The shelters were buried over 3ft in the ground and then covered with a thick layer of soil and turf. Anderson shelters were free to those with an annual income of less than £250 which certainly applied to my parents.

Soon after the move to Essex and seven years after her last child, my mother became pregnant. I suspect this was a great surprise to both my parents. On 10 June 1944, I arrived, my parents' tenth child and their first and only son. I like to think I was the result of Mum and Dad having a cosy night in the air-raid shelter avoiding Hitler's bombs, although I think few of these ever landed in Pilgrims Hatch. More likely is that my mum and dad's visit to the shelter was driven not by fear, but by the desire to have a little time alone together away from their daughters. I may be being rather too romantic here given that such shelters could be very damp, cold and lacking in space. But I hope that for my parents, romance overcame discomfort and that I was truly conceived in an air-raid shelter.

(Incidentally, I was born on the same date, day not year, as the dear old Duke of Edinburgh. For some time as I grew up, I enjoyed the kudos of the stirring music played on the early radio news each 10 June to celebrate the Duke's and, I imagined, my birthday.)

If my arrival into the family was a surprise for my parents, it was a far bigger surprise for my six sisters, even perhaps for the youngest, Vera, who was only seven years older than me. I suspect there were several secret conversations amongst all of my sisters about the shocking implication of my birth, namely that my mum at age 44 and my dad at nearly 50 were still having sex! Even worse, the result of their behaviour was a boy. I cannot, of course, remember how my sisters treated their brother when I was a baby but I have the suspicion that they may have resented me a little because at times when my mum was busy, they would have to look after me and perhaps even take me for walks in my pram. But stories I was told later in life that they occasionally forgot to bring me home from these walks were, I think, apocryphal.

After I arrived, the sleeping arrangements in our house were, Mum, Dad and baby me in one of the larger bedrooms, my sisters Iris, Pat, Connie and Vera in the other normal-sized room and my sister Hilda (whom it seems nobody liked much) squeezed into the 'wardrobe' bedroom which was just about large enough to take a single bed but had virtually no storage space. My eldest sister Joan had left home by this time and married an ex-sailor named Ted; they lived in a house about 200 yards or so from the rest of us.

Mum and Dad shared a double bed, and I slept in a cot. Four of my sisters also shared a double bed in their room, by being packed in 'three down' and 'one up'. I think they operated a lottery system to select which space each occupied although I think there were plenty of grumbles and arguments on most evenings about who should have the 'one up' position; claims about smelly feet often led to trouble I was told.

Picture 2: My mum and dad in about 1949

Money

The move to Pilgrims Hatch meant that my dad could no longer work at the sugar factory, and so he had to spend his time trying to get work locally as a painter and decorator for which he had little experience; much of the time he was unemployed. Mum had not worked since she married Dad. In the new house, her energy was given to keeping the family together and providing as much as she could for her children given the often-limited amounts of money coming into the house from my dad's efforts. Occasionally, she would do some house cleaning work in our GP's house and for one of two other middle-class families she met there. Bringing up a large family on limited income must have been hard although I can't remember really being aware of being poor until I was a teenager.

Earliest Memories

I have heard that some people claim to remember being born; I do not. But when I was about three years old, I distinctly remember being very scared of an extremely loud noise in our garden when I was in the kitchen with my mum and my sister Hilda. I must have been severely distressed because Hilda picked me up and gave me a cuddle in an attempt to stop me crying and screaming. As far as I can remember, this was the only time Hilda took much notice of me and certainly the only time she showed me any real affection. The noise that had upset me was the result of a number of men dismantling our air-raid shelter using pneumatic drills.

Picture 3: An air raid shelter similar to the one in the back garden of 8 Broomwood Gardens in the War.

Another specific early memory is from when I was just over four years old. Dad and my only brother-in-law at the time, Ted the ex-sailor married to my eldest sister Joan, took me to the cinema to see the film of the 1948 Olympic Games which had been held in London (a minor miracle given the state of the UK only four years after the end of the War). Brentwood had two cinemas, The Palace and the Odeon. I think we may have gone to the Odeon. The cinema was, I remember, crowded, but fortunately given later events, we sat at the gangway end of a row which was empty. Sometime into the main feature, I needed to go for a wee; attempts were made by my dad to try to persuade me that I could wait. I was only four and I could not. But neither my dad nor Ted, the brother-in-law, had any intention of missing any of the film by taking me out to the cinema toilet. Instead, they pointed to the wall at the empty end of our row and said I could wee there; I was four years old so I did. I have no memory of anybody complaining, so perhaps the film goers of Essex thought the cinema wall was as good a place as any for a small child to take a leak.

Again, when I was about four years old, I had to have my tonsils out. At the time, virtually all children had this operation. I was sent to Brentwood District Hospital and can remember very well how scared I was when I was put on a trolley and taken to the operating theatre. My fear increased when the horrible rubber mask was put over my face to deliver the gas to send me to sleep; the smell was sickening, and I think I cried until the anaesthetic took its effect. After the operation was over, I was kept in overnight which I think I quite enjoyed because the nurses were so sweet and caring and there were lots of toys and other children to play with.

Chapter 2

Growing Up in Broomwood Gardens

As the 1940s turned into the 1950s, I gradually became more aware of the things happening in my life. These were the days when the country was still recovering from the deprivation of the War years; sweets, for example, were still on ration and anyway the money to buy them was in short supply in my family. My two eldest sisters, Joan and Iris, had now got married and moved out of Broomwood Gardens although they both lived relatively close by. Sister Hilda lived at home but had very little interaction either with me or my three youngest sisters, Pat, Connie and Vera. Eventually, Hilda amazingly also found a husband and she too left the house and moved to Romford; few tears were shed on her departure.

Picture 4: My sister Joan

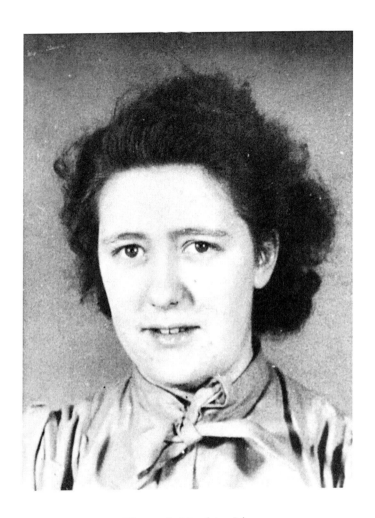

Picture 5: My sister Iris

Picture 6: My sister Hilda

Pat was coming up to 17 years old, Connie to 15 and Vera to 13; three teenagers whom I see, in retrospect, were prototype 'Essex Girls'. Lots of the conversations between the two older girls involved boys, and Mum was not happy with this or with the clothes Pat and Connie started wearing. She also complained about their excess use of makeup. Rows arose about them being out too late, particularly Pat who had left school and had a job in a sweet shop in Brentwood. These must have been troublesome times for Mum; a pregnant teenager in the house would be regarded by neighbours as a clear indicator of loose morals amongst the Everitt girls. And as contraception was still largely hit-and-miss and 'the pill', which would eventually make life simpler for many teenage girls and their mothers, was still a decade or so away, for Mum, no sex was the order of the day for her teenage daughters. On the whole, Mum fought (and eventually lost) these battles on her own; Dad was a mostly silent observer of what was happening. I can't ever remember him raising his voice to anybody in the house despite Mum's prompting that he should.

To the chagrin of my three teenage sisters, Mum hardly ever told me off and was constantly praising my efforts to help her in the house, although as far as I remember these efforts were rather small. But I liked it when Mum gave me 'errands'; running to get a pound of broken biscuits at the Co-op shop about a quarter of a mile away was my favourite as I was always rewarded with a handful of biscuits on my return. About the only time Mum was really cross with me was if I failed to return from the Co-op with a little piece of paper saying how much had been spent there. These pieces of paper recorded all the money we had spent at the local and any other branches of the Co-op by simply giving the shopkeeper our Co-op member's number which I remember was 885302. Every six months, the Co-op then paid out a dividend to its members. I know Mum relied on this dividend to help to get by on what I presume was Dad's meagre and somewhat irregular wages.

Picture 7: My three youngest sisters, Connie on left, Pat in the middle and Vera on the right. The adorable baby is of course me!

Picture 8: Me aged about three

Mum's treatment of me as the dutiful, well-behaved son, did not always go down well with Pat, Connie or Vera. That they thought me spoilt and largely a waste of space was, perhaps, not surprising, but it meant that although I had six sisters and three still living in the house, I probably spent a lot of the time on my own, similar in many respects to being an only child. How did I amuse myself?

Books, the Library, Newspapers and Comics

I guess many only children and quasi-only children such as myself would keep themselves busy by reading. Sadly, the only book in our house seemed to be *Pears Encyclopaedia* which I loved to look through, trying to learn by heart many of the facts it provided but it was somewhat limited as reading matter. (I suspect there may have also been a Bible in our house, but if so, I was never offered it as something to browse for which I remain thankful).

I longed for adventure stories or stories that would make me laugh. Fortunately for me, Mum introduced me to the Brentwood Library although I'm not sure how this came about; perhaps I asked for some reading books as presents and she thought the library would be cheaper?

Going to the library on my own or with a friend became one of my treats from about the age of six. I found *Treasure Island*, the *Just William* books and *The Famous Five* books by Enid Blyton, now of course, frowned on as not politically correct. But I loved the stories of the adventures of Julian, Dick, Anne and Georgina (George), and their dog, Timmy. And the descriptions of the holidays they took that led to these adventures were also wonderful for me. Imagine going to the seaside on their own, having cream teas and loads of fizzy drink. But this was fiction; I didn't know any child in our road who ever went on such holidays, and I never did. The *Just William* books were very funny with all the adventures of William and his pals Douglas, Henry and Ginger (who together were known as The Outlaws), particularly their constant run-ins with William's family, especially his grown-up siblings, Ethel and Robert. William was 11 when the first *Just William* book was published in 1920 and remained the same age throughout the series. In fact, all the characters in the book were locked in the time warp that was the 1920s.

The books I borrowed from the library were initially works of fiction, but gradually I investigated what else was available. Books on how to play various sports, particularly cricket and tennis, attracted my attention as did books on science, especially astronomy. And Paddy, a friend of my brother-in-law Ted, had taught me how to play chess. I found there were lots of books about the game and many of them showed games played in the past between champion chess players, Grandmasters as they were called.

I think you were limited to only four books so choosing took a considerable time, the longer the better for me as I loved being in the library. Taking my books to be stamped and then jumping on the bus home (a 339 I remember) ended each library trip which was always a little sad.

Returning home with my chosen books, I had to find a suitable place in the house to start to read them. This was not always easy. My sisters were mostly very loud, took up a lot of space and did not entirely approve of me reading all the time. 'You'll end up needing glasses,' they would tell me. Or if they glanced through a book about, for example, the Solar System, they would let me know what they thought; 'Doesn't look very interesting to me' was generally their opinion on most of the science books I had borrowed from the library. My sisters were also dismissive of my attempts to learn the notation used in the books I had about chess to describe games played in the past. Once I had picked this up, I was forever playing through the games using my rather flimsy plastic chess set which Paddy who taught me the game had given me as a present.

Some of my sisters' girlfriends who came to visit showed a little more interest in me and my reading matter, even once or twice in how to play chess. But their visits could become tricky when my, usually quiet and unassuming, Dad wanted to show them his war wound; this would have involved him slightly dropping his trousers, but Mum and my sisters were usually quick off the mark to prevent such an indiscretion.

Mum and Dad had noticed that lots of the books I borrowed from the library were about astronomy, space and science, and they must have thought that my interest in these topics should be encouraged. So, when I was about eight years old, they asked me if I would like them to buy me a book covering science in general. I was very excited, and this excitement became even greater when they bought me a three-volume work entitled *Junior Science*. This became my 'Bible', and I loved the diagrams of pulley systems and the pictures of the planets and other astronomical objects. I suspect Dad had raided his savings tin, a syrup tin with the top soldered shut, a slot in the top and screwed to the floor of the cupboard under the stairs, to buy *Junior Science*. Not sure what my sisters thought of this very generous present from Mum and Dad to their 'little boy'.

Although my parents owned only one book, they did take a daily newspaper, the *News Chronicle* and then on Sundays, the *News of the World*. I suspect the *News Chronicle* was centrist in its politics and its editorial position broadly supported the British Liberal Party. I find it rather surprising that it was my parents' choice as they were both staunch Labour supporters who should have been readers of the *Daily Herald*. But the *News Chronicle* it was. (It's rather sad to ponder that when the *News Chronicle* folded in 1960, it was taken over by that right-wing rag, the *Daily Mail*.)

My parents' Sunday paper, the infamous *News of the World*, is perhaps a predictable choice as it provided a little saucy entertainment that might help to liven up the usually dull Sundays that the family often had to endure (see later). The paper was after all also known as the News of the Screws!

As an eight-year-old and later, I was an avid reader of both papers. The *News Chronicle* had great articles on sport, particularly on cricket. I think reading such brilliant articles about the sport was what began my love of the game and to me becoming a life-long cricket fan. One such article which I particularly remember is that on a test match between England and Australia in which Alec Bedser bowled superbly to win the match; 'Lion-Hearted Bedser' was the heading for the article.

The other great attraction of the *News Chronicle* for me was the *Big Chief I-Spy* column. As far as I can remember, you could join the I-Spy club and receive various goodies of which most important was the code breaker book that enabled you to understand the coded message from Big Chief I-Spy in each of his (or perhaps it was her?) columns in the paper. I can't really remember what each decoded message was about; the primary interest for me was the coded nature of the message rather than the contents of the message. It soon become apparent to me that the code book provided by Big Chief I-Spy was not essential as the codes were relatively simply to break without the book. But it became great fun

33

communicating with friends in code, particularly codes which were my own invention; these were far tougher to decode than those of Big Chief I-Spy.

Associated with the I-Spy column were the I-Spy books. These were books covering a variety of topics, for example, cars, animals etc. The *I-Spy Cars* book, for example, contained drawings of many makes of cars with beneath each drawing a space to fill in the date you had seen the car. Each car spotted attracted a number of points, less for say a Ford and more for something a little more exotic, for example, a Rolls-Royce. My friends and I would sit in a tree overlooking the Ongar Road, the nearest 'large' road to Broomwood Gardens, and wait eagerly for each car to pass; in the 1950s traffic was light and this gap could be considerable. There were occasional arguments about the type of car that had just passed by. I suspect the driving force behind such arguments was the cars not yet marked off as seen in a person's I-Spy Cars book. But, on the whole, we all realised that such behaviour was cheating and rightly frowned on if uncovered.

Picture 9: I-Spy Sports Cars, 1955 (Thanks are due to Simon Robinson easyontheeye@wordpress.com)

When you had collected either 1250 or 1500 points (1500 was the maximum and only achieved if every car in the book had been registered as seen) the book could be sent to Big Chief I Spy. If you submitted a book that scored 1500 points, you would be awarded a feather, first class; for 1250 points the award was again a feather, but now a second-class feather. I assume that having both first and second division awards was to allow children who had honestly achieved 1250 points and had little chance of seeing the remaining rather rare cars, to get something for their efforts. Perhaps it was considered that this would help to prevent the filling in as seen, cars that in truth had not been.

The other device designed to discourage such cheating was that before a book was sent to Big Chief I-Spy, it had to be signed by one of your parents to verify the truth of what you had seen. This may have worked well amongst children with middle-class parents, but in Essex amongst the working class, persuading parents that you had indeed spotted every car in the book including say an Aston Martin and a Ferrari was often rather easy. Certainly, my parents were very obliging, and I eventually had a large set of first-class feathers. Fortunately, my friends' parents seemed equally obliging so there were rarely any accusations of any of us cheating or doubt expressed as to when somebody had seen, for example, a Rolls-Royce.

On Sundays, trying to recover from my mum's Sunday lunch (see later), I sometimes settled down in the afternoon for a quick read of the *News of the World*, usually on the lap of my snoozing dad. The sports articles were what I generally went to first, but occasionally I would find myself reading an article where the reporter (normally a Mr. Ron Mount – yes really) described visiting an establishment where women removed their clothes in front of an audience of men including Ron. I learnt that these places were called strip joints. At some strip joints, women apparently offered members of the audience more personal attention. I wasn't completely sure what this meant, but it was clear from reading Ron's column that 'decent' society should and probably did frown on such places. Dear old Ron Mount was at pains in his article to stress that he, of course, turned down what was on offer and left.

Other reading matter I could access came in the form of a weekly comic which I was allowed. My choice was *The Eagle* which I chose primarily to read the illustrated adventures of Dan Dare, Pilot of the Future which were always on the outside cover of The Eagle in 'full stunning colour' as the adverts for the comic told us. Dan Dare and sidekick, Digby, saved the Earth from a whole host of aliens in their long career, but my favourites were 'The Treens' who lived on Venus and were led by the fiendish 'Mekon' who had an enormous head to contain his huge brain and moved about on a levitating chair. The Treens were green in colour and were constantly attempting to take over or destroy the Earth but fortunately never did thanks to Dan and Digby. At the time, nothing much was known about Venus, and as it was about the same size as the Earth and not too close to the Sun, there was speculation about possible intelligent life on the planet. The Treens then seemed not too outlandish apart, perhaps, from their colour. It was therefore a grave disappointment to me when I learned that the surface temperature of Venus had been discovered to be about that of the melting point of lead and that rain fell in the form of sulphuric acid. Even green Treens were unlikely to be able to cope with these climate problems.

Picture 10: Front cover of the first edition of the Eagle Comic in April 1950 (Reproduced by kind permission of the Dan Dare Corporation Limited www.dandare.com).

Radio

Although my interactions with my sisters were largely perfunctory, we did all like to listen to the radio. Fortunately, we all largely agreed on what was a 'must' program to listen to on our elderly and large radio. The weekly *Goon Show*, *Hancock's Half Hour* and *Life with the Lyons*, could not be missed. My mum and dad were also happy to listen to these shows although I think their appreciation of Spike Milligan and Harry Secombe in the Goons was minimal.

Amazingly, the whole family also listened to what was my absolute favourite series, *Journey into Space*. This started being broadcast in 1953, and it was quite brilliant. The three main characters were Captain Jet Morgan, Doc Matthews and Lemmy, the radio operator who had a strong Cockney accent. In the first series, they went to the moon where they encountered 'The Time Traveller'. What followed was a series of journeys into deep space and some travelling backwards and forwards in time. It really was the most exciting event of the week particularly for a boy becoming obsessed with astronomy, space travel and the like.

The programme did, of course, occasionally reflect the social divisions of the day. I can remember vividly one episode where after encountering the Time Traveller by sounds coming from outside their rocket, they were eventually confronted face-to-face with him (her?). Clearly the sight was very, very shocking, but Jet and Doc simply gasped at what they were seeing and stood their ground. However, Lemmy, the Cockney radio operator, screamed loudly but just managed to shout, 'Blimey, I'm off,' before running away. The little episode was a clear demonstration of the writer's belief in the stiff-upper lip possessed by the likes of Jet and Doc, both officers and clearly members of the upper class, and the lack of this quality shown by the clearly working-class radio operator, Lemmy.

My younger sisters and I also listened to music on the radio because there was only a wind-up gramophone in the house which produced rather weird sounds when playing the few '78' records we possessed. And most of these records were eventually used to make flowerpots by heating them in the oven and moulding them into an appropriate shape. But in the early 1950s, the music we heard on the BBC was hardly exciting; Guy Mitchell with *She Wears Red Feathers* and Alma Cogan with *Bell Bottom Blues* did their best but never really touched a nerve in any of us. For me, the excitement that music could provide eventually came later in the 1950s first with Frankie Lymon and the Teenagers singing *Why do Fools Fall in Love* and then with Elvis and *Heartbreak Hotel*. The impact of Elvis, in particular, can hardly be overstated. For me, his music was a revelation as it was for millions of others in the UK. All of us had never ever heard anything so immediately appealing and exciting and which took us out of the general boredom of our lives. *Variety* magazine passing judgement on rock and roll in 1955 said it will all be gone by June. They were wrong.

Nearly 70 years later when I hear Elvis singing *Heartbreak Hotel* on the radio, I have to stop and listen before weeping a few tears over the loss of Elvis combined with a strong memento mori moment. He really was the King.

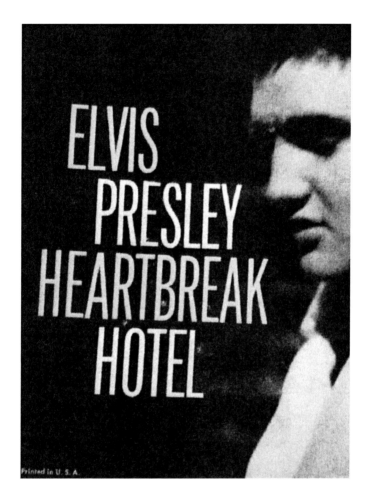

Picture 11: 'The King', Elvis Presley

Television

We never acquired a television when I was a child but one of my friends had one early in the 1950s. All I remember being invited to watch on it was the Coronation of Queen Elizabeth II. On the day of the Coronation, my parents, my three younger sisters and several other families were invited in to watch this important event. The coverage was in black and white as colour TV was still in the future. The screen was about 12 inches square. Everybody that was invited, about 15–20 people I think, were seated as near to the TV as was possible, with children like myself on the floor. The floor was uncomfortable and the Coronation long and hard to follow on the small black and white TV. There was much fidgeting amongst the younger members of the audience, at least amongst those that managed to stay awake. Eventually the grown-ups became fed-up with the children's obvious ennui and they were allowed to go out to play which was probably a great relief for young and old alike.

Sorry Queen.

Food and Meals

Mum did most of the cooking in the house and meals were produced at all sorts of odd times, depending largely when people arrived in the house hungry. My dad always had his 'tea' when he arrived in from work (when he actually had some work) at about six o'clock. My three younger sisters usually arrived home at different times so rarely ate together. I sometime had an evening meal at the same time as my dad but often earlier at about five o'clock after arriving home from school.

On reflection, Mum was not a great cook possibly not even a very good cook. She had far too many things to cope with in her life to concentrate on cooking. Consequently, the meals served up for lunch or supper were never that memorable, although I do remember her suet pudding as one of the best dishes I have ever tasted. Cooked for several hours in the same copper tank in which she did the washing, a slice of Mum's syrup pudding with lashings of golden syrup was something to savour. Nobody since has been able to cook me a suet pudding that gets even close. Mum's bread pudding was also to die for.

And in Mum's defence, she was always cooking in a house with several children around and on limited income. I suspect that food shops at the time were not stuffed with a vast variety of different foods; the aubergines, courgettes, mangos, kiwi fruit and the rest that we are now faced with when we visit the local supermarket were almost certainly unknown to my mum. Even pasta, the staple ingredient of many 21st century meals was, I suggest, not something Mum would have seen in the shops she used, even the co-op, and then during the 1940s there was of course rationing of many foodstuffs to cope with.

Some of the things we were given to eat would now not be considered suitable by the food police, but sugar sandwiches during the day and bread and milk with sugar just before going to bed were our treats, as were the cups of cocoa laden with sugar served up at various times of the day. The common feature of these treats was the sugar, and we all developed a sweet tooth. Sadly, this eventually had its downside for my sisters who hardly ever went to a dentist unless suffering severe toothache; they all had false teeth by the time they reached their late forties. I was more fortunate because I was taken, often kicking and screaming I remember, to a dentist at about the age of seven and every three or four years after that. So, although I still view a visit to a dentist with trepidation, I do have all my own teeth at age 75.

Mum and Dad consumed endless cups of tea when they were both in the house, but I don't remember them ever changing to coffee although I had noticed that there was, in the maid saver in the kitchen, a bottle labelled 'Camp Coffee with chicory'. The few visitors we had were offered tea or coffee, and one or two chose the coffee option; nobody had a second cup when offered. I suspect Camp Coffee was an acquired taste and one that most people preferred not to acquire.

Despite the difficulties faced by the housewife cooks in the 1920s, 30s and 40s, I have to be honest that cooking was not Mum's forte. This became very clear each week when my parents, my three younger sisters and myself sat down to the only family meal of the week, Sunday lunch; this and Sundays themselves were something my sisters and I had to endure.

Sundays

My mum and dad were not in any real sense religious and never attended any church. But apparently respectability demanded that on Sundays I could not play in the street or in the front garden, and my sisters were also confined to the house until late in the afternoon. Each Sunday morning began with Mum preparing the Sunday lunch with the rather unenthusiastic assistance of my sisters. Vegetables had to be prepared early and then cooked for several hours; 'al dente' was not yet a term in vogue in British cooking. And long cooking was also demanded for the meat, most often beef because at the time this was available relatively cheaply as the result of some trade agreement with Argentina. At about 12:30, we all sat down together to eat and attack the meat and

44

veg that Mum had spent the morning cooking. It was not until my late teens that I discovered that slices of cooked beef need not have the toughness of shoe leather nor need be chewed for several minutes before being swallowed. And the vegetables that swam about on the plate could have been tackled with a straw.

Lunch was accompanied in the background by the radio broadcasting *Two-Way Family Favourites*; this was a programme which involved playing records requested by wives and sweethearts in the UK for husbands and boyfriends serving in the Forces and stationed in Germany. The link to Germany was often difficult to hear because of interference on the radio, but the music formed a useful background to lunch, where conversation hardly flowed, although my sisters were fond of making jokey comments about some of the messages sent by the couples to each other which were often a little over the top.

Meat and veg was generally followed by pudding of some sort which was generally far better than the main course. The appearance of one of Mum's wonderful syrup puddings helped to make everybody more cheerful at least for a short time. But thoughts quickly returned to the many hours of Sunday that remained and the associated boredom still to endure; it was difficult to remain cheerful for long.

When the pudding had been consumed, my sisters and I cleared up and piled everything that needed washing up at the side of the single kitchen sink. Dishwashers were some way in the future. My sisters took turns with the washing part, and I dried things as well as I could. Finally, everything was returned to a cupboard or a drawer. Mum and Dad snoozed by the fire during all this activity in the kitchen.

The chore of washing up was made more tolerable by having the radio on blaring out 'Wakey-Wakey' which was the opening of the *Billy Cotton Band Show* or *Educating Archie*, a radio show where the star was a ventriloquist with a dummy called Archie; we certainly never saw the ventriloquist's lips move! The brilliant *Hancock's Half Hour* was also, at times, the after-lunch entertainment.

The next couple of hours were spent facing up to the difficult task of digesting lunch before Mum would suggest it was time for a cup of tea and some of the fruit cake she had made on the Saturday. My sisters and I tried to make our excuses, but a piece of Mum's cake, which only seemed to come in extra-large slices, was mandatory.

During the lengthy tea-time cake eating we were condemned to listen to *Down Your Way* in which an Eaton or Harrow-educated BBC presenter interviewed people from some town or village in the UK. The interviewer asked a series of banal questions clearly constructed to be understandable even by the most ill-educated interviewee. You could not, of course, see any forelock touching on the radio, but I'm sure it was there as the poor interviewee tried his or her best to deal with the snotty-nosed interviewer. After an interview, the presenter would ask Mr or Mrs Country Bumpkin to select a piece of music; the choice was almost always some marching band or some incomprehensible folk song. Eating my mum's cake to this background was a weekly trial; time passed very slowly. (You have to take into consideration that my comments about *Down Your Way* are based on what I remember from listening to the program as a six or seven-year-old someway through the Everitts' ritual and generally boring Sunday. I'm sure some of the interviews carried out by presenters Stewart MacPherson and Richard Dimbleby were quite interesting and neither were educated at either Harrow or Eaton.)

After tea, my sisters were sometimes allowed to escape probably to meet boyfriends, but they had to be back by 9:30 pm. When they had left, I often tried to get radio Luxembourg where the music was far more lively than the music heard on the BBC on a Sunday evening. Sadly, Luxembourg could only be heard with the ear placed against the radio's speaker, and even then, the background noise on the radio was usually overwhelming. But the radio was often the real saviour during each family Sunday.

Each Sunday ended with me taking my weekly bath. Sunday was my day because my sisters were usually otherwise engaged; on other days I had what I think was called a 'stripped wash' in the kitchen standing in my pants and vest, the latter being de rigueur in the 1950s. The bath took time because the temperamental geyser had to be given time to fire up; even then I ended up sitting in about three inches of tepid water, and I was glad to get into my pyjamas and then to bed, which until I was about six was still in the same bedroom as my parents, which was not ideal. Watching my dad climbing into his truss each morning was not the greatest way to start the day.

Heating

In the summer, the routine of getting to bed on a Sunday and on other days was mostly fine, but in the winter, everything changed. Our house had no central heating. This was true of most houses in the 50s and certainly true of the houses of all my friends. In our living room, there was a fireplace which in the winter had a coal fire for heating. As long as you were sitting in one of the armchairs on either side of the fire, everything was fine and cosy, but the heating of the room provided by even a roaring fire decreased rapidly as you moved a little further away. The other downstairs room, the 'front room', was only heated at Christmas time, again with a coal fire.

In the hall and upstairs, the only heating was in the two main bedrooms, and this came from small gas fires built into a wall. Mum considered these too expensive to run except in the severest of winters and then only for half an hour or so before getting into bed. Even when these small fires were allowed, the heating of the bedroom was minimal. In the winter, leaving the relatively warm living room to go upstairs to the lavatory required a great effort of will, followed by a speedy exit from the living room, and then a race up the stairs and along the landing into the bathroom. The return journey to the warmth of the living room was made equally rapidly. Mum would complain of all the noise and racing about, but her complaints fell on deaf ears. The need to get up the stairs to the bathroom and back before freezing to death was a powerful driving force.

In the winter, the bedrooms would have provided ideal conditions for a polar bear, but for my sisters and I the cold was very unpleasant. A shortage of blankets to put on all our beds exacerbated the problem, and most winter nights, we had to resort to putting overcoats (if we had them) on the beds for extra warmth. Bed socks and extra nightwear also helped but not that much. In winter, mornings getting out of bed into a room where there was, occasionally, frost on the inside of the windows often took a great effort of will except from my parents who seemed to ignore most of what my sisters and I saw as the hardships of life in Broomwood Gardens.

Visits to the Doctor

As a child, I was very rarely ill enough to warrant a trip to see the family doctor, a man who, if not quite God, was very close. But on those rare occasions where I had some illness or other that Mum considered should be investigated, she would take me on the bus to see Dr McCulloch who was our family doctor throughout my childhood. Prior to the visit, I was scrubbed and dressed in my best clothes, warned to be on my best behaviour and told to speak up if questioned by the doctor.

The visit began by sitting silently in the waiting room before being called into the doctor's consultation room complete with couch, curtained-off area and life size skeleton (really). The doctor then asked me what was wrong, and it seemed to me that whatever I said, headache, tummy upset, feeling sick etc., he proceeded to examine me in the same way beginning with the stethoscope then a look in my ears with a torch and finally making me open my mouth and say 'aaah'. The examination almost invariably led to a diagnosis that required treatment with a 'tonic'. A prescription for this was scribbled out by Dr McCulloch and handed to my mother who then thanked the doctor profusely and apologised for taking up his valuable time. Mum and I then took our leave, not quite touching our forelocks but close. Then before taking the bus home, we made a trip to the chemist's shop to pick up the tonic, which was generally a bottle of some coloured liquid of which I had to take a teaspoon three times a day. It nearly always worked, and I was generally better in two or three days. Reflecting on such visits in later life, they clearly demonstrated to me the power of the placebo effect!

My friends and I being children of the 1950s never suffered from the allergies that seem to blight the childhood of so many children of the twenty-first century. At many junior schools nowadays, for example, children joining a school have not only their age and date of birth recorded in a register but also a list, not infrequently a lengthy list, of their allergies, and teachers are taught how to deal with reactions to these allergies, some of which can be life threatening. I have no idea why there has been this dramatic change but I like to think that it is maybe due to increased parental pressure on today's children, and the less time they spend scrabbling around in fields and council rubbish dumps than my friends and I did when playing in Broomwood Gardens or in Weald Park (see later).

Boyfriends

I was about six or seven when my sisters Connie and Pat started to bring boyfriends around to the house. Boyfriend and relevant sister were allowed to spend time together in the front room but only on the understanding that I should be in the room with them. The loving couple played cards or some board game with me for an hour or two until my mum had to go out on some errand. Then I was persuaded to leave the room by money changing hands between boyfriend and me; usually a two-shilling piece or a half-a-crown was the cost of my absence. I had to swear not to tell my mum to which I gladly agreed; it was an easy way to supplement my meagre, often non-existing pocket money.

Future events did lead me to question whether I had done the right thing; my sister Pat, for example, married her boyfriend when she was just about 18, and gave birth to her first child about three months later. She had a further seven children by this man but sadly it turned out for Pat to be a marriage made in hell rather than in heaven.

Devon Loch

From the time I was six years old, I began a tradition in the family which lasted a few years and that was to run a sweepstake on the Grand National. This involved getting my sisters and parents to buy a ticket for a shilling to get one horse in the race; in some years, depending on the number of horses in the race, some people, usually my parents, had to buy more than a single ticket. Then I wrote out the names of the horses on slips of paper; these slips of paper were then placed into a suitable bag. Next, I wrote the names of all those who had bought a ticket again on slips of paper; these slips also gave the number of tickets the named person had bought and were placed into another bag. (On reflection, it is not too surprising that I became a statistician later in life).

Following this preparation came the excitement of the draw which took place with the help of my mum or dad. From the bag containing the names of the people playing, a slip of paper was drawn out, and I recorded the name on a sheet of paper. Then from the bag containing the names of the horses, a slip of paper was drawn (or slips if the person had bought more than a single ticket); I then recorded the names of the horse (or horses) that a person had been allocated. On the morning of the race, the allocation of horses to people was revealed to my sisters (my parents already knew, of course). Over the next few hours waiting for the race, the tension rose. Just before the race was due to begin, most participants settled down in our living room to listen to the race which was always broadcast on the BBC.

In 1956, I had bought one ticket, and the horse I was allocated was Devon Loch. The horse was owned by the Queen Mother and was ridden by Dick Francis, later to become a bestselling author. A description of the last part of the race taken from Wikipedia follows:

Devon Loch went to the front of the race with three jumps remaining, cleared the last half a length ahead of E.S.B., and took a commanding lead on the final stretch. Then, in front of the royal box just 40 yards from the winning post and five lengths ahead, he suddenly inexplicably jumped into the air and landed on his stomach, allowing E.S.B. to overtake and win. Although jockey Dick Francis tried to cajole the horse, it was unable to continue. Afterwards, the Queen Mother said: 'Oh, that's racing.' It is not known why Devon Loch jumped; some reports claimed he suffered a cramp in his hindquarters causing the collapse. Another report asserted that a shadow thrown by the adjacent water-jump fence (which horses only traverse on the first circuit of the Aintree course) may have baffled Devon Loch into thinking a jump was required and confused as to whether he should jump or not, he half-jumped and collapsed. Jockey Dick Francis later stated that a loud cheer from the crowd, for an expected royal winner, distracting the horse is a more likely explanation. Reports that the horse had suffered a heart attack were dismissed, as Devon Loch recovered far too quickly for this to have been the case. He lived another six years, being put down during or shortly after the cold winter of 1962–3.

Picture 12: Devon Loch falling in the Grand National 1956;
note that there is no fence to jump!

It is hard to describe how I felt. I had been thinking of how I would spend my winnings just before the radio commentator shrieked that the horse had fallen. But there were no fences left to jump, I thought, so he must be mistaken. Sadly, there was no mistake; E.S.B had won. E.S.B had been allocated to my sister Pat. She showed no inclination to share her winnings with me despite my best efforts to persuade her that this would be the Christian thing to do, a mistake on my part given the lack of this or any other religious leaning in my family.

This was the last year I ran the sweepstake.

Pigeons

In the early 1950s, Dad suddenly became interested in pigeon racing which is the sport of releasing specially trained pigeons which then return to their homes over a carefully measured distance. The time it takes a bird to cover the specified distance is measured and the bird's speed is calculated and compared with all the other pigeons in the race to determine which pigeon returned at the greatest speed.

I suspect Dad had come across a couple of men who belonged to the local pigeon club when he was on a painting job, and they persuaded him to get some pigeons and join the club. Having decided to go ahead with this, the first task was to build a pigeon loft at the bottom of the back garden well away from the house. Dad and his new-found friends managed to construct a quite impressive loft over the course of a few weekends helped by a constant supply of tea and cheese sandwiches provided by Mum.

Next, of course, was to acquire some racing pigeons, and Dad bought several from the other pigeon fanciers, but I never found out how much money changed hands. I did notice however that the syrup tin in the cupboard under the stairs had been raided.

Having the pigeons and the loft in which to house them, Dad was ready to join Brentwood's Pigeon Racing Club. But before Dad's pigeons could race, they had to be trained. Training involved taking them in a wicker basket increasing distances away from the house and then releasing them. Here Dad was helped by another pigeon-racing enthusiast who had a car. Waiting for them to return from these training flights was an anxious time for Dad and me. But return they generally did, settling first on the roof of the house and then encouraged to fly into their loft by Dad and me shaking tins of millet. In general, the birds were quick to leave the roof and enter the loft.

After the pigeons had been in training for some weeks, Dad decided it was time to enter a couple into a race. This involved taking the chosen birds down to the club on a Friday evening and having them 'ringed', meaning essentially each bird being given an identifying rubber ring which was attached to the bird's leg. When the bird returns to its home, the ring has to be removed and placed in a slot in a special clock which records the time that the bird arrived back. From this timestamp, an average speed is measured, and it is this speed that is used to place the birds in the race. The identifying number of each pigeon is recorded and the clock set and sealed.

Next, all the birds from the club entered in the race were put in a couple of large baskets and taken to Brentwood Station. Here they would be transported by train to the start of the race which might be anything from 100 to 500 miles away.

Sometime on the Saturday morning after the baskets containing our pigeons arrived, along with all the other birds from other clubs in the race, all the baskets were opened and the pigeons released, presumably by a member of the railway staff trained for this job.

Then on Saturday around about lunchtime, Dad and I would place ourselves by the loft with our tins of millet ready to shake as soon as the birds appeared. My anxiety, and I suspect Dad's, began to rise as time passed without any sign of our birds. But eventually they appeared on the roof, and after much shaking of the millet in the tins, the hungry birds made their way into the loft relatively quickly. But once in the loft, they had to be caught and their rings retrieved so we could 'clock' them. Dad had become pretty good at this as he knew the clock was ticking and every second might make a difference. But occasionally, catching a bird and removing its ring could be frustrating, and although Dad rarely swore in the house, in the pigeon loft on a Saturday afternoon, he often came up with number of new swear words, which later I might use to impress my friends. After all the birds we had entered into the race had returned and their times had been recorded in the clock, Dad and I would return to the house for a cup of tea.

On the Saturday evening, a visit to the club was needed so that everybody's clocks could be unlocked and the speed of each pigeon in yards per minute calculated. Winners were congratulated and others consoled. Prizes for the winners and runners up of all the different races that club members participated in over the year were presented at an end of year club 'dinner and dance', an event not to be missed. Mum and I would attend with Dad, all smartly dressed and my hair heavily laden with Brylcreem. First, there was a sit-down meal with, I suspect, lots of cheap wine and sherry being consumed. The main course was generally chicken which, for me, was a treat. After the meal, there were speeches and then the presentation of prizes: cups and a small monetary prize for winners, certificates and an even smaller monetary prize for runners up. Dad won several certificates over the years. At the end of each year's event, we generally took a taxi back to Broomwood Gardens, a small sample of the high life for the Everitts.

Picture 13: Second prize certificate awarded to my dad for a pigeon race in 1956.

Grandparents and Other Relatives

By the time I was born, Dad's parents had both died so both my grandparents were from my mother's side. But sadly, they were almost as good as dead to me. I met my grandad only twice before he died. Once was in Broomwood Gardens when he arrived one day having simply left his care home in Thurrock, which was about ten miles or from Brentwood. He and I didn't have much of a conversation because he was mostly involved with Mum, explaining I suppose why he had left the care home. Not much came from the conversation except Mum was adamant that Grandad had to return from whence he had run away. Next day, Mum took Grandad back to Thurrock by bus, and I saw him only once again when Mum and I went to visit him back in the care home. I think he died a few years later.

My maternal grandmother, I never met. I am not sure Mum had much to do with her; she had after all sent Mum away from the family home in Ramsgate to live with an aunt when she was only three. But I understand that Grandmother was quite a sparky character who ended up marrying at the age of 76 a man twenty years younger.

The only relative of Dad I ever met was his sister, my Auntie Flo. She lived in Walthamstow in East London, and Mum and I went to see her a couple of times travelling by bus from Brentwood. She lived in a very small house and we sat around a small boiler in the kitchen having tea. Auntie Flo had a daughter Carole who was a few years older than me, but she was quite friendly and so time didn't drag as much as it might have. Auntie Flo must have died in the next few years, but I do not remember my parents going to her funeral.

Christmas

The first Christmas I can remember is when I was between four and five years old. I remember Christmas Day as being just wonderful. When I woke up, I found that Father Christmas, whom I had met some weeks before in Gamages having been taken there by my sister Iris, had left a pillowcase full of presents, mostly toys with the odd packet of sweets and a tangerine or two. Searching through the pillowcase was very, very exciting, and I was very grateful to Father Christmas.

As I got a little older and Father Christmas faded into the mythical figure he is, I was fortunate enough to get even more presents in the pillowcase at the end of the bed than in my earliest Christmases. I then started to question how my parents had managed to afford this. I came to the slightly concerning conclusion that it may be related to my sister Pat having a job in a sweet and toy shop in Brentwood. At first, I thought she had been able to buy the presents I was given very cheaply because she was a member of staff. But after more thought, I began to link the number of Christmas presents I was given with the abundance of fireworks I had on Bonfire Night; I always had a large number of all types of fireworks from bangers and jumping jacks to large roman candles, and my friends and I had a great time letting them off in the road. Pat's shop also sold fireworks. It seemed to me that either Pat was being given the presents and fireworks free by the owner of the sweet shop or she had helped herself. This worried me a little but what could I do? Later in life, I learned that my suspicions were correct; Pat told me that she rationalised her behaviour by comparing her wages with the takings in the shop. How did the owner not discover what was happening?

Having visited Pat in the shop a number of times, I think the middle-aged, balding owner had a soft spot (and perhaps a less than soft spot at times) for her. Pat was a very vivacious redhead, lively and with a great sense of humour. She eventually left the shop to get married; Christmas presents for Brian suffered.

Christmas dinner (well lunch really) was always a special occasion in my younger days. There were Christmas crackers and Christmas pudding with silver threepenny bit coins hidden inside. I always seemed to get a piece of pudding that included one or even two of these coins which was very exciting despite my sisters muttering about Mummy's boy always being lucky. And the crackers provided hats and little gifts such as whistles, dice and the like.

The afternoon was spent playing with my presents or some board games with whatever sister stayed awake. Mum and Dad would usually retire to their bed for a little sleep, at least that's what I thought it was for. Sometimes they would join us for a few games and then Dad would take a small shovel, fill it with chestnuts, and toast them over the fire; delicious!

At about five o'clock, Mum started bringing out the port wine, beer and soft drinks in preparation for an evening with a few friends and the rest of the family. As I grew a little older, the 'family' would include my married sisters along with their husbands. Dad lit a fire in our front room where there was a large and real Christmas tree surrounded by presents for all and sundry.

When people arrived, they would be directed to the front room where Mum would pass around slices of Christmas cake and mince pies, thankfully baked by my eldest sister Joan who was a rather good cook. Everybody would congregate in the front room around the Christmas tree. Once everybody had arrived and been supplied with drink and cake, I was allowed to give out the presents. Presents for me, and there were lots, I left in a pile that I could investigate later. Gradually, the discarded paper from all the presents being unwrapped became a fire hazard so Mum would stop proceedings before we all became engulfed in flames and remove the mound of torn up paper to the rubbish bin in the kitchen.

My brother-in-law Ted would always have a 'fun' present for Mum which he had specially constructed. One year, the present consisted of a series of wooden boxes arranged like Russian Dolls, with inside each box a key to the next one; the final box contained some epigram about mothers-in-law which I failed to understand but everybody else thought funny, particularly Mum, who by now had consumed two or three glasses of port and lemon; given that she never drank alcohol except on Christmas Day, she was perhaps a little tiddly.

After all the presents had been given out and admired or otherwise, people divided into card players and non-card players with the former shuffling off to the living room leaving everybody else to remain in the front room. By the time I was about eight, I was allowed to join the card players in exciting games of 'sevens' or 'Newmarket', made even more exciting because we played for money. The players included Dad, sister Joan and her husband, Ted, and at various times, some of my other sisters and their respective husbands.

The room quickly filled up with cigarette smoke as most of the players were smokers particularly Dad and Ted who always had a thin roll-up cigarette on the go. Mum never played cards but kept the players supplied with snacks and booze. The room had all the aspects of a serious session of card playing, but this was somewhat undermined by the size of the stakes, pennies, half-pennies and even the odd silver threepenny bit. The games were generally very light-hearted and fun. The only exception occurred when I lost all the money I had started with. This led to a few tears which always worked in persuading Mum to bankroll me so I could continue playing. More tears were sometimes needed if, at the end of the session just before people were leaving, my pile of coins was much smaller than at the start. Generally, as intended, this made most of the players (not my three youngest sisters) drop a few of their coins on to my pile so that it gradually grew larger than the one I started with. Later in life, this behaviour was the subject of much ribbing by my relatives.

I loved these Christmases and as a child assumed that everybody else loved them as much. But when I was about ten, I began to be aware that some of the company, particularly several of my sisters and their husbands were plainly out of sorts with each other; snippets of overheard conversations like 'I told him lunch would be at one and he didn't arrive back from the pub until two-thirty more than a little drunk' alerted me to the far from ideal partners some of my sisters had married. The future showed that my conclusion was not too far from the truth.

The Lodger

When only my three youngest sisters were living at home, Mum started to take in lodgers who slept in the small bedroom once occupied by my sister Hilda. This room was really small, but there seemed to be no difficulty getting lodgers; a civil engineer working on a new reservoir project and a young man who had been taken on as a trainee golf professional at Brentwood Golf Club, were two lodgers I remember.

Mum advertised she had lodging available in several places including at the wireless station which was about two miles away. One day, a young man who was due to start work at the wireless station arrived at the door and asked Mum whether a room was available. At the time, Mum was having a rest from lodgers who usually ate an evening meal at our house and made considerably more work for her. Mum told the young man politely that no room was free. He was also very polite and said he understood why Mum would not take him as a lodger; the young man was black or a 'man of colour' (the current but ridiculous politically correct term). Mum quickly picked up what he thought, namely that this was a 'no coloureds lodging'. Mum called the young man back and said that he was welcome to have the room despite her having a little rest from taking in people. I suspect this was the first black person Mum had ever met face-to-face, but she needed to make it clear to the young man that his colour was not the issue when first telling him the room was not available.

The new lodger was called Ray, and in addition to being black, he was also from the USA. He stayed for about three months and became popular with everyone. Ray was very good looking, so my sisters were forever vying for his attention; he treated them politely but never stepped over the line except perhaps occasionally making fun of them but in the nicest way! Dad liked talking to Ray about pigeon racing; Ray was very patient. And I loved Ray because he was interested in science, and he told me about his course at the wireless station which involved learning a lot about radio transmission and radio waves. He also taught me a little of the mathematics he used.

Ray became one of the family, and as Christmas came when he was close to completing his course, he joined the Everitts for Christmas lunch. I think he enjoyed the experience, and it was a wonderful day for all of us, particularly for me as Ray bought me a Christmas present, a kit for making things from sheet metal and strips of metal by using the cutting tool included in the kit. Also included in the box was a small booklet of things you could make with the kit. Ray and I chose to make a soap rack that you could hang over the side of the bath. After about an hour of cutting and bending, we had in front of us a stylish (perhaps a tiny exaggeration) soap rack which we took upstairs to the bathroom, hung it over the bath and placed into the tray a bar of soap.

Everybody was impressed but sympathised over the several cuts to our fingers Ray and I had suffered; the metal strips in the kit were unfortunately razor sharp. Because of the wounds Ray and I had suffered making a simple soap dish, Mum decided that the kit should be put away until I was older. I never saw it again. The soap dish was used for a few days so as not to upset Ray although I think he would have simply greeted the soap dish being confined to the dustbin with a smile.

The same Christmas I was also given another present Ray and I enjoyed together. This was a small trumpet modelled on Eddie Calvert's 'golden trumpet'. Eddie was a well know musician at the time whose gimmick was to play a gold trumpet. My trumpet was also 'golden' but after Ray and I had used it for sometimes trying to play the tunes in a little tutor book that accompanied the trumpet, the gold very rapidly disintegrated leaving a rather less attractive trumpet to perform on. And it has to be said that neither of us showed much talent as trumpeters and the trumpet was soon confined in a box of old toys that were rarely played with. But it was fun while it lasted.

We were all sad when Ray had to leave and return to the USA. After he had left, Mum received several odd letters through the post each of which contained only a piece of black paper. My suspicion is that some of our neighbours were making a point about having a black man in the road. I like to think that despite these troubling letters, had any more such men arrived at our door looking for a room, Mum would have taken them in. I think her example certainly helped my three younger sisters and myself to avoid developing into racists which I suspect was a rare boast amongst people in our road and probably for the vast majority of the population of Essex then and now.

Shopping in Brentwood

When I reached the age of about six, one or other of my youngest three sisters would be detailed by Mum to take me into Brentwood either to buy me some new clothes or to take me to the library, sometimes both. This trip involved a bus ride on a 339 which I always looked forward to. The library was always the most exciting stop on this trip and whichever sister I was with often made it clear that we had spent quite enough time looking at books. If clothes buying was on the agenda, I was dragged to some shop; I can't remember which but possibly a branch of the Co-op. I took little interest in my clothes but Mum had given accompanying sister a list of what I needed: a new jumper, shirt or pair of short trousers perhaps. But when I was about eight, my sisters took me on a shopping trip but completely ignored Mum's list. Instead of my normal clothes, I was dressed in a check shirt, waistcoat, jeans and a rather gaudy tie. I thought I looked pretty good, 'cool' perhaps, although the word had not been invented then. Unfortunately, Mum was unimpressed and cross words were exchanged with my sisters. But with the passing of a few days and backed up by Dad who thought my new outfit was quite dashing, Mum relented, and I was allowed to wear my new clothes on certain special occasions.

One trip to Brentwood that I remember clearly was to watch the opening of the new Brentwood Arcade. The Arcade housed a number of new shops particularly more up-to-date clothes shops for younger members of both sexes. I think I went with Pat and Vera. I suspect they were both excited about the possibilities of buying their clothes somewhere more exciting than the rather drab and non-fashionable women's clothing stores in Brentwood High Street that they had been forced to patronise so far.

The Arcade was to be opened by Barbara Lyon. Barbara was a member of the Lyon family who with parents Ben and Bebe and brother Richard, starred in a radio series called *Life with the Lyons* which began in 1950 and ended in 1961; it was the first situation comedy in the United Kingdom. Barbara Lyon was extremely glamorous and the show she was in, very popular. The result was that a large crowd were outside the new Arcade wanting to see her. From the balcony, Barbara appeared looking very glamorous indeed with a hat the likes of which I had only ever seen before in pictures in the newspapers. The crowd cheered and Barbara gave a speech the gist of which I have forgotten but I do remember the last sentence, 'Now you won't have to go to Romford for your shopping,' Romford being a larger town about six miles or so due west of Brentwood which ran a market on Wednesday and Saturday. The cheers for the speech were muted and the elderly ladies near me muttered, 'We will still have to go to Romford for the market.' But Barbara had done her best and left the balcony. A great day for all *Life with the Lyons* fans of which I was one.

Picture 14: Barbara Lyon

Chapter 3

Trips and Outings

Unlike the children in the *Famous Five* books, I never went on holiday during my childhood; I guess money was simply too short for such luxuries. I can't say I ever felt deprived as none of my friends seemed to go away on holiday either. But I was taken on a few trips and outings that I still remember very well.

To the Seaside

My brother-in-law, Ted, married to my sister Joan, acquired a van which had seats for the driver and one passenger and then room in the back for several people to sit on the floor. On several occasions, this van was used to take Joan, Ted, Mum, Dad and me to Southend for a day out. Southend is about 40 miles east of London and was at one time the favourite destination for a day out for hundreds of East Enders.

From Pilgrims Hatch, where we lived, Southend is about 25 miles away, but the journey took at least a couple of hours in the van and it was pretty uncomfortable on the floor in the back. But the trip was special for me because Southend was so exciting.

First there was Southend Pier, originally opened in 1889 and extended in the early 1900s and again in 1927, with the final addition being made in 1929. At this time, the pier was 1.34 miles long, making Southend Pier the longest pleasure pier in the world. The more energetic day trippers would walk to the end, but we took the little train that ran backwards and forwards to the pier end. The train was similar in design to those used on the London Underground. I loved riding in the train to the end of the pier.

Picture 15: Southend Pier

Southend also had one of the earliest theme parks called the Kursaal. The entrance hall led to a longish walkway on both sides of which were penny-slot machines. Inserting your money into one of these machines caused it to spring into life with the action depicting perhaps some historical event or other, for example, the beheading of Anne Boleyn, or the hanging of Dr Crippen. Executions seemed to be a speciality, and although scary, they were also fun. And you could, of course, see a beheading or hanging that you particularly liked, several times, simply by inserting another penny. There was also a 'Laughing Policeman' kiosk which I'm afraid I found to be rather dull.

At the end of the walkway, you came out into the open where all the rides were situated. There were roundabouts, ghost trains, chair-a-planes, bumper cars and others on which the riders screamed a lot but appeared to be having a good time. The only one I sampled was the bumper cars with first my dad driving followed by Ted; it was wonderful. Mum and Joan were invited to take a ride, but they never did; both were far too nervous.

The Kursaal was closed in 1970, and much of the land was developed as housing. Fortunately, the entrance hall, being a listed building, remains but now contains a bowling alley arcade and casino rather than the penny machines I remember so well; a great loss, I think.

Picture 16: A view of The Kursaal Southend-on-Sea from the air.

Before getting back into the van to return home, we might eat fish and chips wrapped in newspaper sitting on the front looking out to sea. Lots of people did the same thing many eating cockles and winkles which I never tried. And 'Kiss-me-Quick' hats were on show in abundance. Sometimes there was no sea to look at, just mud flats; the tide at Southend took the sea out past the end of the pier. After fish and chips, Rossi's ice cream was usually on the menu, as were several cups of tea for each of the grown-ups; after each cup, Ted and Dad would smoke a cigarette. Eventually it was back into the van for the journey; I think I slept most of the way.

Very occasionally, the trip to Southend would be made by train and then my three youngest sisters would also come along. When we arrived on the beach, Dad would take up his place on a deckchair and snooze and smoke. I would go to paddle and watch my sisters swimming; I really wished that I could swim. After being in the sea, we would get down to making a sandcastle with even Mum joining in. My three sisters were great company for me on such days out. I think it was a relief for them to get out of Broomwood Gardens and have some fun with Mum and Dad and even with their little brother, who most of the time at home was a constant irritation to them.

Such memorable trips to Southend either by van or by train were probably the reason I was never jealous of the holidays taken by the *Famous Five*.

On rare occasions, and as a very special treat, Ted and his van took us to Clacton which was about 60 miles away and, like Southend, was predominately geared to catering for working-class holidaymakers although it had some more 'select' areas aimed for the lower-middle classes. This trip became an adventure which took much planning with sandwiches and drinks packed into the back of the van and even cushions to sit on. Dad couldn't drive and so Ted insisted on at least two stops for cups of tea on the way. I suspect the journey took about three hours in each direction so time in Clacton was limited. We usually went to the beach and possibly hired deckchairs. I couldn't swim and neither could any of the adults, so we contented ourselves with a paddle at the edge of the sea. Dad and Ted would roll up their trouser legs to the knee, and Mum and Joan held their skirts up to just above the knee; there was much giggling and splashing, and I think everybody had a great time. I was often pushed over by Dad or Ted so got completely soaked, but it was all great fun.

After all the activity, everybody was ready for lunch and so the egg sandwiches were opened and consumed, soft drinks taken, and many cigarettes smoked by Dad and Ted. Days in Clacton were enjoyable, but for me never really compared to a trip to Southend.

Picture 17: Brian about seven paddling at Clacton

I also went on a trip to the seaside town, Walton-on-the-Naze, with a group of other children when I was about seven years old. It was organised by the Rotary Club of Brentwood, and several of my friends came too. The Naze is a peninsula north of the town which is important for migrating birds and has a small nature reserve. Walton is not far from Clacton, and we travelled there in some antique bus which was very slow and uncomfortable. But the journey was still fun with my friends, and when we arrived after about three hours motoring, we were all allowed to go to the beach and paddle; none of us could swim yet. We enjoyed the sea and then built sandcastles. Cricket on the beach followed and then lunch supplied by the Rotary Club which was very good.

In the afternoon, we were given an hour to explore the pier. Walton's pier was rather shorter than the one at Southend, but it did have a number of amusements such as machines with cranes which you manipulated via wheels on the outside of the machine and attempted to pick up one of the toys in the bottom of the machine. This seemed easy until you tried operating the machine and nobody managed to extract anything from the machine despite several attempts by each of us.

In our exploration of the pier, one of us came upon something that was instantly interesting to everybody. The find was a variety of '*What the Butler Saw*' machines. The machine had a viewer that you looked into and was operated by a handle at the side. With your face in the viewer and a turn of the handle, you could view a woman gradually undressing until she had nothing to remove; all the machines showed much the same event but with different women and different outfits to remove. This was fascinating stuff for eight-year-old boys, and we all had several looks into the machines until our money ran out.

On the bus home, the '*What the Butler Saw*' machines were the subject of some very giggly conversation and they were certainly the high point of our trip to Walton-on-the Naze. We never discussed the migrating birds.

Picture 18: What the butler saw machines as used on the pier at Walton-on-the Naze.

(I have to confess that there is evidence from the photos I have from my childhood that at some time, my parents, my three youngest sisters and I went to Ramsgate, the town where Mum was born. Perhaps we went there to meet our maternal grandparents, but I simply have no memory of the trip at all which is a great shame. The evidence is provided by the word 'Ramsgate' scrawled on the back of Photograph 19, but unfortunately no date is given. The photograph clearly shows my three youngest sisters, my parents and me, on what must be Ramsgate beach. Mum and Dad have settled into deckchairs, and the rest of us have obviously been busy building a sandcastle. It looks like it was fun.)

Picture 19: Some of the Everitt family on the beach at Ramsgate about 1948

Trips to the 'Flicks'

Brentwood had two cinemas in the 1950s, the Odeon and The Palace. The Odeon was built a little way off the High Street because of the remains of a chapel dedicated to St Thomas the Martyr which was a protected building. The Odeon was the classic 30s cinema in which the circle foyer had a large ring of Art Deco lighting in the ceiling. The Palace cinema was perhaps a little more downmarket than the Odeon but not quite down enough to be rated as a fleapit. Sadly, both cinemas are now just a memory with the Odeon being closed in 1974 and Palace in 1968.

The Odeon ran a Saturday morning club where young kids like me could go in free to watch adventure films. These were most often Westerns of which my favourite involved the *Thunder Riders*. These films all had similar plots in which brave and handsome cowboys killed lots of cowardly Indians. The noise of the audience reacting to what was happening on the screen was generally deafening. I loved these Saturday mornings but realised later in my life how stereotyped were the characters in the films and how prejudiced against the Indians were the plot lines.

For some reason, my mum used to take me to one or other of the two cinemas almost every Friday. We went to the early evening show at about six o'clock. I think the outing was a reaction to Mum never being able to persuade my dad to go to see a film. Anyway, Dad's loss was my gain. Looking back, the confusing part of my cinema trips was that Mum never bothered to check the time a film started. The result was that we would often take our seats in the dark some way through the story being played out on the screen before us. And as in those days the show was always a two-hander, we would sit through to the finish of the film we came into, see the next film from beginning to end and then see the part of the first film up to the point when we arrived. Now this seems crazy, but at the time, I thought it was fine; being out with Mum rather late by the time the show had finished was exciting. And there was, of course, always the ice-cream in the interval bought from the tray carried by a pretty young usherette. The two adjectives here may not be entirely accurate, but as I have grown older, I have continued to think of cinema usherettes in the 1950s as both pretty and young. (By this stage in my life I had, fortunately, found out the appropriate place to go for a wee when in the cinema.)

Picture 20: The Odeon Cinema Brentwood.

First Trip to London

In 1950 when I was six, my sister Iris took me on a train into London and then on the underground to meet Father Christmas. In fact, we met him twice on the same day. First, we went to the large department store Gamages which was near Holborn. The store no longer exists. Here Iris paid half-a-crown for me to see Santa. I remember that I got to sit on his lap for a few minutes, but I was far too shy to say anything to him in answer to the usual banal questions about what I wanted him to bring me for Christmas. But as he sent me back to Iris, he gave me a small package as a pre-Christmas present which was exciting. Iris took the package and said I couldn't open it until Christmas Day which seemed a bit harsh, but I didn't make a fuss – well, perhaps a little fuss. Sadly, the present from Father Christmas got mixed up with all the other presents I was given on Christmas Day, and I have completely forgotten what the present was that I had been given by Father Christmas.

From Gamages we travelled on to Selfridges in Oxford Street. Amazingly so did Father Christmas because we met him there again. In Selfridges, Santa had a sidekick called Mr Holly who was entirely dressed in green. Here no money changed hands for visiting Santa which was good; on the other hand, he had no presents to hand out to his visitors. But Iris did buy me some sweets in Selfridges which I suspect must have been very expensive.

On the long journey home to Broomwood Gardens, I fell asleep on the train from Liverpool Street to Brentwood and possibly dreamed of Christmas Day that was now so close.

A Second Trip to London

In 1951, the Festival of Britain took place. Intended as a 'tonic' for the nation, this festival of culture, art and science took place on the South Bank in London. The Festival focussed entirely on Britain and its achievements and was funded chiefly by the government, with a budget of £12 million. Amazingly, this festival was so highly regarded even Mum and Dad were persuaded to pay it a visit and they took me along; I was seven.

The two things I remember most about the festival were the Dome of Discovery and the Skylon. The first of these featured the largest dome in the world at the time standing 93 feet tall with a diameter of 365 feet. The theme of the exhibition in the Dome of Discovery was 'British initiative in exploration and discovery is as strong as it ever'; this was after all the Festival of Britain so perhaps a little return to Empire and flying the flag was excusable. The exhibition was divided into several sections including Polar, Sea, Sky and Outer Space. The latter was particularly exciting for a seven-year-old interested in astronomy and space travel. However, I managed to get lost in some exhibit or other where it was very dark. I was very frightened and cried a little until Dad found me.

Picture 21: Dome of Discovery, Festival of Britain, 1951

The Skylon was next to the Dome of Discovery. It was a futuristic-looking structure, a vertical cigar-shaped tower supported by cables that gave the impression that it was floating above the ground. To me, the Skylon looked like a rocket, and I think I believed it was a rocket for many years after our visit. I often pondered on why it never flew.

Picture 22: The Skylon, Festival of Britain, 1951.

After looking around the main festival sight, we took a boat for the short trip along the river to Battersea Park which was home to the fun-fair part of the festival. There were many exciting rides including a water chute which started by taking riders seated in a small open carriage upwards, a bit like on a roller-coaster, and then plummeted them downwards, eventually crossing a small stretch of water where riders were splashed by the resulting wave before the carriage that they were in was brought to a halt. There was much screaming from the people taking the ride and much drying off when they exited the ride, mostly laughing at the experience they had just had. Mum, Dad and I watched for some time, but I don't think there was ever any question of us taking the ride, for which I was thankful. I was far too nervous a child to think that a ride on the water chute might be fun.

A memorable day out.

Another Visit to London

One Saturday towards the end of the first year in my secondary school (about which more later), I remember going on a trip into London with Gary, who was in the same class as me. Gary and I were both keen bus number collectors, and so equipped with our Ian Allen's bus number books and several pens, we travelled on the tube to various London locations where we could see lots of buses, take the number displayed on the side of the engine cover and then, assuming we hadn't seen the bus on any previous trip, underline that number in the relevant Ian Allen book. Just before the time Gary and I went on this trip, London Transport had introduced one or two of the new 'Route Master' buses on the No 2 route between Crystal Place and Golders Green. Gary and I thought the chance of us seeing one was remote. But then, late in the day, standing in Trafalgar Square, what should come from the direction of Leicester Square but a bus number collector's dream, a shiny new Route Master with the number RM1. I'm not sure about Gary but in retrospect I think this was the first genuine orgasmic moment in my life. It was a bit like finding a penny black in your stamp collection.

A Trip to France

Like many comics of the time, there was a club associated with *The Eagle* that readers could join for a small fee sent as a postal order. I can't remember much about the advantages of being a member except that you could go free on certain trips if accompanied by two paying adults. Sadly, as it turned out, I took up this offer and arranged a boat trip from Southend to Calais for Mum and sister Iris. So, with me clutching my Eagle member's card and Iris holding on to the tickets for the two adults, we set off by train from Brentwood Station to Southend. To catch our boat to France, we had to go to the end of Southend Pier, the longest pier in the world at over a mile long. We took the little train that ambled backwards and forwards all day to the end of the pier to catch the boat.

Arriving at the end of the pier, we made our way down a gangplank to board the boat. I would like to claim it was called HMS Eagle but it wasn't, and I have forgotten just what it was called. My mum, Iris and I found a place to sit on the deck as it was a reasonably pleasant day. We watched as the ship left the jetty and started to make its way to France. At first, everything went well mainly because we were still in the Thames Estuary and the water was very calm. I knew that the water would get far less settled as we got into the English Channel and said so, but Mum reminded us, not for the first time, that she was the daughter of a Kent fisherman and so rough seas held no concern for her. About half-an-hour later, this claimed advantage of being a fisherman's daughter looked less than convincing as my poor old mum suddenly felt rather ill and did indeed vomit over the side of the boat. By this time, spray was making conditions impossible on the upper deck and so the three of us made for the lower deck which was covered. But downstairs was very stuffy and reeked a little of fresh vomit both from our own 'Fisherman's daughter' and the many others who were not quite as good sailors as they would have liked. The smell and the lack of fresh air then made me sick; fortunately, Iris proved that the gene for never being sea-sick might have missed my mum but had been inherited by the daughter of a daughter of a fisherman.

Arriving in France an hour late meant that the coach tour we had booked was somewhat curtailed. Iris and I had to help Mum on to the coach still clutching a sick bag from the boat, fortunately one that was still empty. The boat took us to see some of the sights of Calais which were less memorable that might have been expected. I cannot remember any of them. But the tour ended at a sweet/cake shop where we purchased a box of what turned out to be rather revolting sweets as something to remember our day out in France.

We climbed up the gangway back on to the ship determined this time to stay on deck for the return to Southend. It rained continuously for the three-hour journey back to England. Mum, however, would not contemplate leaving the deck open to the rain for the shelter of the lower deck despite the concern shown by the odd member of the crew who passed the sorry sight of two very wet women and a similarly afflicted young boy. She thought moving to the lower deck would cause the return of her sea sickness. I thought the same would happen to me, so I was happy remaining on the open deck.

Back in Southend, we took the train back to Brentwood where Iris insisted on taking a taxi back to Broomwood Gardens. Back in the house, we dried out, and Mum who had not felt sick on the return boat journey said how much she had enjoyed what turned out to be the only day in her life spent outside the UK. I was not convinced.

A Day of Fishing

Our next-door neighbours in Broomwood Gardens were a Mr and Mrs Neubar who I think were the only people in the road who owned their own car, an Austin 10. Mr Neubar enjoyed fishing, and one day when I was about six years old, he asked my mum whether I might like to join him for a day's fishing (I don't think the Neubars had any children of their own). This was the early 1950s, so my mum didn't ask to see his DBS certificate but simply put the idea to me, and I must have said I would love to go, because one sunny morning, off I went in the Austin with Mr Neubar.

We drove to the River Roding, about six or so miles away. I helped unload the fishing equipment, and we took a short walk through a five-bar gate on which was the notice 'Private Fishing for Members of the Ongar Fishing Club' to the river. Mr Neubar had brought two rods, and he helped me get one ready to fish before attending to his. Then we fished. I soon had a bite and with Mr Neubar's help landed a small perch which we removed from the line and placed in a keep net. Nearly seventy years later, I can still remember the excitement that this first small success gave me. As the day progressed, we landed quite a few more perch, some of which seemed to me quite large. We may have caught other types of fish, but I only clearly remember the perch. What we talked about, I can't remember exactly, although I suspect it was mostly about fishing and maybe a little about how I liked being at Pilgrims Hatch Primary School (see later).

After a couple of hours fishing, we stopped for lunch. Mum had given me cheese and tomato sandwiches which were my favourite, and she had also packed a bottle of Tizer which Mr Neubar and I shared. After eating, we returned to fishing, and then at about 4 pm, we packed up and drove back to Broomwood Gardens. There were other days I joined Mr Neubar to fish but I remember this first day as one of the most perfect days of my childhood.

(Mr. Neubar was bald; according to my mum he became bald when a bat flew into his hair and was then removed by shaving his head. Although I did think this rather odd, I was at an age when I believed what Mum told me and I was always rather nervous when I went into the back garden in early evening where there were always bats flying about. Of course, as I got older, I realised that Mum's story was a figment of her imagination, and by the time I reached twenty my fear of bats causing me to become bald had all but been extinguished.)

Chapter 4
Friends and Play

Friends

I was fortunate that from about the age of five, there were several boys of the same age living near our house in Broomwood Gardens. Robert lived in the house opposite; he was an only child and his parents were a little posher than mine. Jack lived a couple of houses away from me; he had two older sisters, Sylvia and Sandra, and a television. Paul lived just out of Broomwood Gardens and he also had two sisters, but I have completely forgotten their names. Robert, Jack and Paul were my best friends, and I spent a great deal of my spare time playing with them.

We were fortunate that Broomwood Gardens provided a perfect place for all sorts of outdoor activities because it was used by so little traffic. Only one or two people in the street owned a car. And as the road petered out at one end into a large stretch of fields which then ran into the council rubbish dump, there was no real reason why cars would use the road. Milk deliveries and bread deliveries were both by horse-drawn carts into the early 1950s so bothered our activities very little, and we all loved to pet the horses. Even as five-year-olds we were allowed to 'play in the street' by our parents, and at this age, hopscotch, hide-and-seek and tag were popular. We also collected and played with marbles which you could buy even with the limited pocket money most of us had. Many of the marbles we owned were really quite beautiful.

At one end of Broomwood Gardens were fields which contained lots of humps and bumps and were perfect for playing Cowboys and Indians particularly for those of us who had suitable clothes and weapons. Fortunately, quite a lot of people had cowboy outfits and some Indian outfits. I had a rather fetching cowboy outfit with a holster and a shiny gun. Those playing Indians would have homemade bows and arrows. The battles were taken very seriously, and there were constant arguments about who had won. It was difficult to decide because the number of participants alive on each side at the end of a battle was the same as when the battle commenced. The arguments quickly died out when we had to return into our houses in Broomwood Gardens for lunch or tea.

As we got a little older, our play involved more and more attempts to copy the sports and to emulate the sportsmen we had read about in the newspapers or heard on the radio. The most popular sport in England at the time was football, but surprisingly perhaps, we rarely tried to play football in the road. Perhaps the road simply wasn't suitable for football or perhaps we had become more interested in other sports. Certainly, the England football team of the early 1950s had been humiliated by Hungary, losing 6–3 at Wembley and so were not perhaps the childhood heroes they might have been.

As six and seven-year-olds and beyond, we used Broomwood Gardens for cricket, tennis, running races and trolley races.

Cricket

Our interest in cricket was sparked by articles in the newspapers about Alec Bedser, Len Hutton and others, and the test matches that England played, particularly those against Australia. And, of course, Essex was (and is) a Cricket County Championship team. In the 1950s, the Essex team travelled to grounds around the county: Leyton, Ilford, Clacton, Southend and Brentwood. The team played two three-day matches on the Brentwood Ground, and myself and one or two friends would take our packed lunches, use our pocket money to pay the entrance price and sit on the grass around the boundary and watch from start of play at 11:30 until late in the afternoon.

Essex was not a great team at the time, but they did have the great Trevor Bailey and Doug Insole who both played for England. Trevor Bailey was England's leading all-rounder after the Second World War and known as Barnacle Bailey on account of his stubborn defensive batting. Doug Insole played for England on a number of occasions and when he retired from cricket become chairman of the England selectors and President of the MCC. Other players I remember were Dickie Dodds, an attacking batsman, and Mickey Bear who was a great fielder.

I suspect that the type of play we watched in the 1950s would have little appeal to young cricket fans nowadays brought up in the era of T20 games. For us, a day watching Essex was special, and on the bus going home, we would go through the events of the day in some detail even when Essex had made, say, 200 for five wickets. I don't think we ever considered the cricket we watched dull or boring. Perhaps our expectations were simply too low? Maybe, but a day out watching Essex in the 1950s was always a treat for my friends and myself.

The 'cricket pitch' we used in Broomwood Gardens was simply across the street from one side to the other, with the wicket being chalk marked stumps and bails on a wall. Only one cricket bat was needed as only one person at a time was batting. Fortunately, one of my many presents one Christmas was a reasonable bat which lasted a couple of years because the only ball we were allowed to use in the street was a tennis ball or similar. Bowling was strictly overarm with the run-up restricted by the space available to two or three steps. Fielders were placed in carefully chosen positions in the road in an effort to protect gardens. Anybody hitting the ball directly into a garden was given six-and-out. Batsmen kept their own scores which was not without its occasional controversy. Once or twice, this self-scoring practice ended the game because of doubts expressed about the veracity of the batsman. But mostly the games were enjoyed by all and I think helped all aspects of our cricket when later played at school. Our fielding, in particular, was improved by the street cricket we played. My own fielding was also helped by the many hours I spent throwing a tennis ball against the back wall of our house and catching the return. The pebble dash on the house did however suffer.

In Broomwood Gardens, cricket was rarely called off for rain.

Tennis

I'm not sure how we got into playing tennis in the road. I think it was a combination of factors. A couple of tennis rackets had been given to one of us; I had learned how to score from a book on tennis from the library, and particular features of the road surface of Broomwood Gardens were perfect for tennis. Firstly, the road was light coloured, almost white really, not tarmac. And running down the centre of the road was a black line crossed at intervals by similar black lines. The road was essentially divided into sets of four squares making it perfect for tennis apart, of course, from the lack of a net in the middle of pairs of squares. But did this stop us? It did not.

We played some good tennis, overhead serves only, with a rule that these must bounce only a little way past the centre line. The net problem was taken care of by having a net judge who called fault if he considered a ball was going into the non-existent net. Again, this was not without its difficulties, and arguments with the net judge could be heated; the odd tennis ball would sometimes be hit in the direction of the judge. Perhaps a similar sort of childhood tennis is what has led Nick Kyrgios to some of his less than attractive behaviour on court?

Running

Running took off in Broomwood Gardens for a variety of reasons: reading about Roger Banister winning mile races before breaking the four-minute barrier in 1954, and hearing about an Essex runner, Jim Peters, who ran marathons in the early 1950s, a feat that we regarded as superhuman. In fact, Jim broke the world record for the men's marathon four times in the 1950s and was the first runner to complete a marathon in under 2 hours 20 minutes, an achievement which was equated to the breaking of the four-minute mile. Both Roger's and Jim's heroics were inspiring reasons to want to run.

My dad also told us about a much earlier runner called Alfred Shrub who was a middle- and long-distance-runner in the early 1900s and who in 1904, at Ibrox Park, Glasgow, broke the one hour run record as well as all amateur records from six to eleven miles, and all professional records from eight to eleven miles, running 11 miles, 1137 yards (18.742 km) in one hour. We had never heard of Alfred Shrub, but he was a hero of my dad, and his running feats were enough for us to add him to our list of running greats.

In addition to these genuine running stars, there was the fictional runner, Alf Tupper, the Tough of the Track, a character from *The Rover* comic for boys. Alf ran mile races on a diet of fish and chips with, apparently, minimal training and he almost always won. We all loved the stories about Alf.

But I think that maybe what persuaded us most that we should run was that one of us had a watch with a second hand so we could 'accurately' time any runs we did.

A number of running events were carefully considered, but eventually we decided on three: a middle-distance race, namely 'once around the block' which was about 500 yards, a long-distance race, 'four times around the block', and the 'cross-country race' which included a section around the council rubbish dump. As there were about five of six boys wanting to take part, we thought all racing together would lead to complaints from pedestrians we were likely to knock over, so we decided to have only one or at most two of us running at the same time. The watch with the second hand used for timing was left with one of the non-runners. All times were recorded in our 'running book' so we could note how we improved and who was best at each particular event. All runs were done in whatever clothes and whatever shoes we happened to be wearing on the day, most often short trousers, shirt and plimsolls.

People in Broomwood Gardens and the close neighbourhood were witness to some heroic running during the early to mid-1950s. Sprints at the end of the 'once around the block' event were often desperate in the aim to get a good time. Near collapse at the end of the 'four times around the block' sometimes brought complaints from a runner's mother or even occasionally their dad. Little did they know that by far the greatest danger to their son was the cross-country run through the rubbish dump over pieces of corrugated metal placed over festering streams of possibly toxic material. Fortunately, nobody ever fell despite the various obstacles encountered, and we all survived our experiences of the cross-country run relatively safely. Today's 'Health and Safety' regulations would, of course, have killed the fun we had with the cross-country run before it began.

Sadly, the book in which all the times for the different races were recorded was lost. But while it survived, it gave all the racers endless hours of pleasure checking their improvement and personal bests over the three or four years that racing took place.

Trolleys and Trolley Racing

In the 1950s, making 'trolleys', vehicles constructed mainly from wooden boxes and old pram wheels, was almost a rite-of-passage for most young boys; it certainly was for myself and my friends. But construction of a good trolley was not easy, and I was fortunate that my dad and my brother-in-law Ted both chipped in to help build my first trolley. They found a suitable box in which the driver could sit, bits of wood for the base and for the axle on which the front wheels were mounted and to which long bits of strong string or rope were attached that allowed the driver to steer. Most importantly, Dad and Ted came up with some old pram wheels that were perfect for what was needed.

My friends also roped in their dads to help with their own trolleys, and after a few weeks' construction time, I think four of us in Broomwood Gardens had pretty nifty machines. We would race them in pairs down the road with other friends pushing to get us going. This was exciting but was often subject to some rather ordinary steering which occasionally resulted in minor and, every now and again, more major crashes. Injuries to drivers were not unknown. But most of the time, the sheer excitement and fun of the races more than made up for the scraped elbows, knees, etc. that were suffered. Someone once said, 'As we have no money, we have to think.' Neither my friends nor I were from families with much money, but we gave much thought to making our childhoods memorable. The trolleys were one distinct step in the right direction.

Picture 23: A trolley: This is very similar to the ones we made in the 1950s but far better made. I saw it in Ruskin Park, Camberwell in 2019. It was being raced about by two children and I asked their dad if I could take a picture which he very kindly allowed. I am very grateful to him.

Garden Play

Although most of my play with my friends was in the road or further afield, there were times when we played in each other's gardens. In my garden, for example, there was a small slope on the path leading from the house to the end of the garden, and we found this was perfect for racing our Dinky toys of which we all had several. My own collection of Dinky toys included mostly cars and racing cars. Little did I realise that if I had kept them in their boxes and never played with them, they would today be worth quite a reasonable fortune.

But I did play with them, and the fun I had racing them against my friends' cars was priceless for a six-year-old.

The slope could also be used, particularly if given a little watering, for snail races (more exciting than you might think!) The snails were first collected from various places in the garden and then lined up before being sent on their way down the slope. Occasionally, some lettuce leaves or similar might be needed to get them to start. But once underway, the snails would progress slowly and not always in a straight line to the winning post which was about 20 yards from the top of the slope. Identifying whose snail had won was not always easy and could lead to lively arguments; mostly these ended in much giggling reflecting the fun we had from such pursuits.

And on occasions, one or other of us would have read something in one of the numerous 'Books for Boys' on the market that sounded interesting and that we should attempt. One of these I remember well involved how to observe ants in their nest. The first thing, of course, was to find a convenient ants' nest which then had to be dug up and placed in a suitable wooden box from which one side had been removed and a sheet of glass inserted. With my dad's help, the box with a glass side was soon available and so we began the search for an ants' nest. Ants themselves were no problem; the garden was full of them. But where did they nest? Luckily, there was a compost heap near the bottom of the garden, and in there, we found what we were looking for. The nest was dug up as best we could (I suspect several hundred ants were left homeless) and transferred to the box. Excitement increased as we could view the ants in action below the surface and the whole experiment was viewed with a certain amount of pride, not just by my friends and myself but also, I think, by my mum and dad.

Sadly, we then became too ambitious and considered that there was room in the box for at least one more ants' nest. We moved to another compost heap in Robert's garden and acquired our second nest which was then deposited in the same box as the first nest. It soon became apparent that the ants from the two nests did not get on with one another and that the merger of the two nests had been a mistake. After a time, our box was largely filled with dead ants, which was a shame, but we had learnt a little about why ants from different nests need to be kept apart.

At times when we were playing in my garden, my dad would bring out his bayonet which he had kept from his time in the Army during the First World War. Usually, the weapon was kept in the cupboard under the stairs but was brought out occasionally to let my friends and I help in its cleaning; this involved little more than thrusting the bayonet into and out of the ground a few times. After the process, the blade gleamed, and we were all allowed to hold it for a few minutes before Dad returned it safely to the understairs cupboard. Dad's bayonet clearly meant a great deal to him and probably bought back some pretty terrible memories of the First World War in which he was wounded.

Pets

My friends and I all had either a cat or dog which could be helpful for garden play. Throwing a ball for a dog to retrieve could be fun but usually frowned upon by a garden's owner with carefully cultivated flower borders to maintain.

Cats were lovable on a lap by the fire but rather dull when asked to provide excitement in a garden.

My garden had the advantage of providing more exciting pets to play with. The first was a grass snake which I think Dad had found in the garden of a house he was painting and brought home. Fortunately, Dad's snake identification expertise meant that the grass snake was just that, not a more sinister type. We all loved holding the snake, and it was certainly more exciting than some lazy cat.

Similar to the grass snake was the slow worm, again found by Dad, this time in the fields at the end of the road. This could be safely handled and when finished with was returned to its 'cage', a large cardboard box. But one day, the slow worm was not in the box and could not be found. I think it had escaped through a small crack in the side of the box. There were no tears however for a lost slow worm; it just wasn't that sort of a pet. But several weeks later, the slow worm was discovered in Dad's compost heap at the end of the garden. It was, of course, dead. Again, there were no tears.

Last of the more unusual pets I had was a tortoise. This would roam about the lawn, and my friends and I would feed it lettuce leaves which was quite fun. But on occasions, the animal would get lost amongst some flowers, so to stop this, we drilled a hole in its shell and attached a piece of string to the tortoise and to a sturdy stick hammered into the lawn. This prevented the tortoise getting lost but was, on reflection, a rather cruel solution to the problem. The tortoise eventually died, perhaps, from having had its shell drilled. We should have treated it more humanely. Just a few tears were shed.

Indoor Play

On the few days when outdoor play was impossible (monsoon rain, thunderstorm or temperatures twenty degrees below freezing), my friends and I played in one or other of our houses. We played board games such as Ludo, Snakes and Ladders and sometimes, draughts. When allowed, more boisterous pursuits like hide-and-seek whiled away the time, but these were often curtailed by one or other parent whose house we were in when he or she couldn't stand the noise anymore.

Sometimes, we compared cigarette card collections of cricketers or footballers and exchanged duplicates for cards we didn't have. A little more exciting was comparisons of our stamp collections. Stamp collecting was almost *de rigueur* for young boys in the 1950s. Packets of assorted stamps could be bought very cheaply from shops such as Woolworths. The stamps would then be carefully mounted in the relevant page in a stamp album. The stamps we had bought were not, of course, rare, but they had their interest; for example, some of the German stamps from after the war costing millions of Marks had us discussing why they had what seemed a ridiculous price tag.

One day however, Mum took me to a sale in the Brentwood Furniture Market which sold mostly cheap furniture but occasionally had a variety of other items probably resulting from a house clearance. While Mum checked out the furniture, I looked around the boxes containing lots of other items, and in one I found a large stamp album. I picked this up and opened it; to my surprise it was full of stamps I had never seen before from countries that I had not come across before. This was exciting, so I found Mum and asked her for a shilling which was what was being asked for the stamp album. She handed over the money, and I quickly became the album's owner. Just as we were about to leave, a man of about thirty approached and told me I was very fortunate to buy the stamp album, the implication being that it was far more valuable than a shilling.

When I arrived home with my new stamp album, I went through it in more detail. There were many triangular-shaped stamps, some of which were quite large, and stamps from parts of the world that I had to look up in *Pears Encyclopaedia*. This was all very exciting, but sadly, the stamps had not been mounted but simply stuck in; there was no way they could be removed without irretrievable damage. The stamp album was a great thing to have bought, but sadly, it was not going to make me rich.

Clearly being indoors was a little boring compared to being outside which is probably the reason that only really severe weather conditions kept us cooped up.

Girls

As young boys in the 1950s, we knew girls existed, but they played virtually no part in our games. Girls, we thought, were sensitive creatures who liked to cook, clean or make clothes, although there was Georgina known as George in the *Famous Five* books who preferred to climb trees, go boating and have adventures; but this was fiction not real life. Occasionally, when three or four of us boys were sitting in a tree discussing life in general, the subject of girls would arise mainly in the context of how unsuitable they were for the games we played. But every now and again, the discussion would focus on our curiosity of how boys and girls were different from each other anatomically. Some of us had sisters, so our information about these differences might have been thought to be more accurate than friends with no sisters. I have my doubts that this was the case. As eight-year-olds, this curiosity about girls was, as I remember, not particularly intense, and certainly not as important as the results in our Broomwood Gardens sports events. But for three of us a situation arose where even our mild curiosity was satisfied.

Towards the end of the road next to the fields, there was a house in which two children, brother and sister Eric and Paula, lived. They were a little older than myself and my friends, with Eric being about eleven and Paula about nine when we were all about eight. In general, we had little to do with the pair perhaps due to the age difference, but more importantly there was something a little bit disturbing about Eric. It is hard to give any clear evidence for this observation except that Eric wore very thick glasses, rarely appeared in the road and apparently had few friends of his own. Even on the rare occasions when any of us bumped into Eric, few words were exchanged.

But one day, Eric approached Jack, Robert and me when we were playing some cricket. I have no memory of how the conversation started but a very clear memory of what it led to. Apparently, his sister Paula was more than willing to show us in close-up how boys differed from girls, as long as, in return, we reciprocated. I suspect there was some embarrassed giggling, but I guess we all decided this was too good an offer to turn down, so we followed Eric back to the kitchen of his house where he summoned Paula. When she arrived, clearly primed for what was required, she proceeded to lift her skirt, remove her knickers and invite each of us to examine what was revealed. For each of us, I think the overriding driving force was curiosity and questions were asked about details and answered by Paula with, as far as I remember, no obvious embarrassment. After about five minutes, knickers were replaced and skirt lowered. Now Paula claimed her reward, and 3 eight-year-old boys undid the buttons of their shorts to each display a rather limp penis. Paula approached a little closer to examine what each of us presented and amazingly took hold of each penis in turn for a moment or two. Penises were then returned to trousers.

The event was over, and we left. On reflection, the strangest thing about what happened was that Eric stayed as an observer. The three of us were rather quiet and never really talked about what had taken place either amongst ourselves or with other friends. Certainly, there was no question of telling our parents. The event was, at that age, driven largely by curiosity rather than by sex which took another few years before it really entered my life.

I could search for all sorts of explanations for what took place and what it implied about the relationship between the brother and sister involved. But this was the 1950s, and as an eight-year-old life rapidly moved on. I simply assigned what I had learned about the difference between boys and girls to my memory as possible useful information to be used in future discussions about that difference.

Paula and Eric, moved away from Broomwood Gardens about a year later. I have no idea where they moved to and I have no reason to believe that their move away was in any way connected with the event described above.

Chapter 5

Weald Park

One of the joys of being a child in the 1950s was the freedom we had to play in the road and to roam into the nearby countryside. Even at seven or eight, I could tell Mum in the morning that I was going out with my friends, and she would simply tell me to make sure I was back in time for tea; she would make sure I had an apple and some sweets to sustain me. Where my friends and I usually made for was Weald Park which was about two miles away down a road called Sandpit Lane, or closer if we crossed nearby fields and ignored the wrath of a local farmer.

These were the days long before the existence of the mobile phones that all children nowadays have so they can keep in touch with their parents and when even telephones in houses were rare. We certainly never had one, and to make phone calls we had to walk about two hundred yards to the nearest red telephone box and struggle with the press button A or button B instructions. Oddly, I can remember the number of our telephone box, Coxtie Green 370, although I used it only rarely. (Memory is sometime very strange.) Parents in the 1950s were perhaps less neurotic about the fate of their children when they left the house. I suspect the lives of both the children and the parents did not suffer from not being in constant touch with each other.

Weald Park

Weald Park is a 500-acre park which originated as a deer park in the twelfth century. In the sixteenth century, the principal building of the park, Weald Hall, was started by Sir Brian Tuke and added to by Sir Anthony Browne in the 1600s. Over the intervening centuries, the park and house were bought by Hugh Smith. Smith employed Capability Brown to carry out landscaping and then sold the park to Thomas Tower, a lawyer who died in 1810. Thomas Tower was succeeded by his eldest son Christopher, who died in 1867 at the age of ninety-two. The park was inherited by Christopher's grandson and then remained in the Tower family until 1946 when it was sold to the Metropolitan Railway Country Estate Company. In the middle 1950s, the park was purchased by Essex County Council who turned it into a country park.

Picture 24: A view of Weald Hall in Weald Park

Nowadays, the park is open to all and continues to provide the potential for a great deal of pleasure for families from far and wide. In the early 1950s when my friends and I discovered the park and its possibilities, things were not so straightforward. The park was essentially private and signposted as such on gates, etc. This made every trip to the park an adventure; we chased and hid from each other always with one or both eyes open for the park wardens we assumed lurked in the park looking for small boys whom they could take into custody with no doubt dire results for all of us. In fact, the only official custodians of the park we ever encountered were of an age and a mobility which precluded them ever capturing us fleet-footed six and seven-year-olds.

The only real danger of being on the receiving end of a cuff around the ears was from the fishermen around one of the lakes in the park. Here 'Private Fishing' really meant something, and any attempt by one of us boys to try to get a bite in the lake with our homemade 'stick and hook' equipment resulted in much verbal abuse and even the occasional chase and some physical punishment if caught; this was usually relatively minor and, in the 1950s, was never enough for us to bother telling our parents about.

Fortunately, when roaming the park, we had come upon a small pond which although containing no fish of interest to serious anglers, did contain newts, tadpoles and frogs which were like manna from heaven to my friends and me. The newts, in particular, were so accommodating, attaching themselves to the hooks on our little rods as if they could hardly wait to exit life in the pond. Once or twice, we put the captured newts into jam jars containing some water and carried them home. This proved to be a poor idea. When back in the house, the newts escaped from their new jam jar homes on to the floor to be found lifeless and desiccated in the morning. My mum was not amused, and in future, newts caught in the pond had to be thrown back at the end of our fishing.

We all loved the days of fishing and exploring Weald Park; it was for a few years a magic place for us all. And when we eventually returned home for tea, or occasionally in the summer, for supper, I suspect we were all pretty hungry and tired. No doubt, a good night's sleep followed, punctuated by dreams of catching a monster newt or escaping from an angry fisherman. These were good days to be a young boy in Essex.

A Search for Bronze Age Artefacts and an Accident

When Weald Park was taken over by Essex County Council and was no longer private, we still often went there, but perhaps the excitement and the magic was a little less than before. Nevertheless, the park still played a considerable part in our lives, and it even arose in one of our lessons at Pilgrims Hatch Primary School (see next chapter) dealing with ancient history in England. According to our teacher Miss Harris, there was some evidence that there had been a Bronze Age settlement in, or at least close to, Weald Park. She suggested it might perhaps be possible to find some artefacts from the period in the park or close by. The prospect was irresistible, and on the Saturday following the Miss Harris lesson, Robert, 'Winkle' (a friend at school but not from Broomwood Gardens, so whose real name I have forgotten) and I made our way to the park to search for Bronze Age treasure.

Sadly, none of us had any real knowledge of how archaeologists worked, and our initial enthusiasm for our task on a very hot day quickly evaporated despite the discovery of what we were convinced were arrowheads; they were not! After a couple of hours, we had a rest to eat our sandwiches and finish our shared bottle of Tizer before giving the search one last chance. Another unsuccessful hour passed, and we then decided it was time to make our way home. By this time, we were all very thirsty, but we had no drink left. This called for a plan which was for one of us to go to the door of one of the big houses close by the park and ask politely for some water.

Rather than all going, we thought just one person would be less likely to spook the owner. After a rather involved selection process of which I have no memory, 'Winkle' was declared the winner (or loser as it turned out). He bravely took up the challenge and started to make his way down the rather lengthy drive to the front door of the house.

Perhaps we missed the 'Beware of the Dog' notice or perhaps there simply wasn't one, but Winkle's walk to the house was interrupted by the appearance of a large, barking dog who proceeded to clamp his sizeable mouth on Winkle's knee causing our hero to scream very, very loudly. I'd like to claim that Robert and I sprinted to the rescue but sadly the truth will out, and we remained stock-still at the road end of the drive, horrified at Winkle's fate but powerless to help. Fortunately, the commotion led to the opening of the front door and the appearance of an elderly lady shouting at the dog to let go of his prey. This dog knew the sound of a voice that had to be obeyed, and Winkle was released, from the dog at least, but still had to face the wrath of said lady who now stood over the weeping, bleeding and very shocked boy. Robert and I made an unspoken decision that it was perhaps safer for us to stay where we were.

After briefly assessing the situation that confronted her, the elderly lady told Winkle to stop making such a fuss (had she never heard of rabies?) and went back to the house. She quickly returned with bandages, water (at last) and two smallish pieces of chocolate cake, one for Winkle and the other as a treat for the dog, presumably for stopping the obvious burglary that Winkle was about to perpetrate. We remained where we were, having, I think, decided that this was not the time to check if there was any more water and chocolate cake on offer.

Winkle was eventually sent on his way, blood-soaked bandage around his knee and clutching a bottle of water; he had rather selfishly consumed all the chocolate cake that had been on offer. He was still a little shocked by the experience, and Robert and I had to help him back along Sandpit Lane and to his house which was a little way from Broomwood Gardens. We could have met his mother in happier circumstances, and it was clear from her reaction to Winkle's injuries that his trips with us to the park would from now on be severely curtailed. In fact, they were ended, and despite the high regard Robert and I had for his heroic behaviour during our boy versus dog incident, Winkle became a more distant friend whom we now only saw at school. I have to admit that Robert and I failed to cover ourselves in glory during this adventure. By the way, the dog was called Sidney.

Chapter 6
School

The Wooden Knitting Needle

For some reason, I was first taken to a school at the age of four which in the late 1940s was unusual, particularly for working class children. The school I attended was the Coptfold Road Infants School which was in Brentwood, about a mile and a half from where we lived. I would like to claim that I walked there and back as a four-year-old, but sadly, I did not. I was taken on the bus, probably by one of my sisters, although memory fails me here as to which one. I remember very little about the school except that even we infants were subjected to physical punishments by the two or three teachers that made up the staff of the school. The most feared of the variety of painful slaps, pinches etc. that were handed out was the rap on the knuckles with a large wooden knitting needle. Seventy years on, I can still remember the pain and the resulting tears. The school is, fortunately, no longer there. In its place is a small art gallery selling a variety of paintings and prints including those produced by Banksy.

Pilgrims Hatch Primary School

I spent about a year at my first school before moving to the school that had been built on the hayfield that backed onto the back gardens of the houses on our side of Broomwood Gardens. The loss of this field for adventures was more than made up for by the arrival of a shiny new school, Pilgrims Hatch Primary, with humane staff including a cheery headmaster, Mr Davies, a man of Wales who, of course, loved singing. As I was to discover, Mr Davies had surrounded himself with reasonably kind and reasonably intelligent staff. Wooden knitting needles across the knuckles became a thing of the past.

Fortunately, most of the friends I had in our road and those in nearby roads started the school at the same time as myself. It's a long time ago, but I think we were all reasonably happy, at least most of the time, and I think the school provided a good educational environment. I happily learnt my multiplication tables which were conveniently printed on the back of our exercise books. Along with these tables were all sorts of interesting measurements to learn about, for example, that a furlong is 220 yards, that there are eight furlongs in a mile and the rod, pole or perch is 16.5 feet and used by surveyors (not sure why!).

I particularly liked the maths lessons and those on science especially when these covered a little astronomy. I loved learning the facts that the teacher reeled off; speed of light 186,000 miles per second, the diameter of the Sun is 864,000 miles, the distance of the Earth from the Sun is 93 million miles etc., etc. Oddly, I can still recall these facts despite the passing of nearly 70 years and that these days I can hardly remember what I did yesterday. In one class, the teacher wanted us to put together a 'newspaper' with the different sections that real newspapers had. I was chosen as the science editor and my desk had a cardboard notice with 'SCIENCE EDITOR' written on it. Other desks had corresponding notices displaying 'SPORTS EDITOR' and 'POLITICAL EDITOR'. My contribution to the class newspaper was an article about the distance to the nearest star and how long it would take to get there travelling at (a) motor car speed, (b) aeroplane speed and (c) rocket speed. There was considerable scepticism that the time taken by the rocket was, give or take a thousand years depending on the type of rocket, 40,000 years. I did my best to explain by telling people that the nearest star was about four light years away, and that light travelled at 186,000 miles per second. After that I asked them to do the necessary multiplication to get the distance to the nearest star in miles. Not many managed the calculation correctly.

I also enjoyed English lessons, particularly writing stories. I think my stories were often quite good, but sadly the spelling and punctuation was poor. In fact, my spelling was so poor that my eldest sister Joan, whose education had not been so hampered by the War as had that of my other sisters, gave me some spelling lessons; she tried hard but with limited success.

One day, I mentioned to one of our teachers, a Mr Roberts I think, that my dad kept racing pigeons. He was very interested and wondered if Dad might donate a few pigeons to the school if a suitable loft was built. I went home very excited about the possibility, and Dad said he would be only too happy to give the school three of his pigeons. So next day, I let Mr Roberts know, and he was very grateful. The only thing left to do was to build the loft. This is where the project started to falter. Mr Davies the Head was happy for the school to provide the timber but building the loft was down to Mr Roberts and the helpers he could recruit from the boys (these were not the days when girls were expected to help with this kind of onerous physical activity). About five of us were very happy to help, and the building work started after school one day. But it soon became clear that Mr Roberts had no real idea of how to construct a pigeon loft, and although there was much sawing of the timber we had, followed by nailing some bits of the cut wood together, there was nothing resembling a loft for pigeons at the end. I think what we had constructed was possibly an early example of an abstract piece of art. After some discussion with Mr Davies, the loft idea was abandoned and what we had built was taken down by the caretaker. What had started out as a brilliant idea ended in a shambles. My carpentry and general DIY skills have not improved with age.

Our headmaster Mr Davies was keen on all aspects of music and theatre, and each year the school put on a 'show' generally at some other school in Brentwood where there was a suitable stage. My only appearance in one of these shows was as a court official in *The Pied Piper of Hamelin*. My only line was repeating 'Rats' several times as the court was invaded by suitably attired boys and girls clearly revelling in their roles, which I have to say were far more exciting than being a dull court official.

Along with academic topics, there was, of course, PT and sports. These were mostly fun with those in the summer that involved cricket being particularly enjoyable; playing cricket in the road had clearly helped my straight-batting technique.

And often, in the time waiting to have a bat, I can remember lying on the grass watching skylarks hovering overhead.

The 11+

In 1955 when I was 11 years old, I had to take the dreaded 11+ examination, the result of which would decide the school I went to when I left the safety of Pilgrims Hatch Primary School. Not passing the 11+ meant I would be condemned to attend Doddinghurst Road Senior School which was where most of my sisters had gone. I think the horror stories I heard about this school from my three younger sisters helped me work hard at school, which led to my passing the exam. Prior to taking the examination, my parents had to list four secondary schools in order of preference that they would like me to attend if I passed the 11+. The school listed as the first preference was Romford County Technical School (RCTS) although I have no clear memory of why this was selected.

Rewards

As a reward for passing the 11+, I remember being given two presents by my parents. The first was an Oxford 'thumbnail' dictionary which I had requested largely because of the thumbnail index rather than any enthusiasm for the dictionary itself, although remarkably I still have and still use the dictionary.

Picture 25: A present from Mum and Dad for passing the 11+.
This is the Oxford thumb-nail index dictionary I was given in
1955 and is still in use today 65 years later!

The second present was a 'working model' space rocket.
I cannot remember who the rocket was made by, but I had
spotted it in a local toy shop and couldn't wait to get my hands

on one; a present for passing the 11+ provided the perfect opportunity. The rocket was powered by a Jetex motor, a type of solid-fuel rocket motor produced for use as a powerplant for model aircraft. The thrust of the engine forced a small rod inside the rocket upwards to keep a hatch at the front of the rocket shut. When the fuel was spent the rod dropped back releasing the hatch and allowing the small parachute kept there to open and bring the rocket safely to the ground for its next flight (at least this was the theory).

The thrust developed by the engine was relatively modest and was only suitable for horizontally launched flying models rather that vertically launched rockets. So, the rocket came with a launch device, essentially a large spring, which launched the rocket on a horizontal path before the thrust from the engine took over and pushed it upwards 'to infinity and beyond'. The theory seemed flawless.

Sadly, when the rocket was taken to a nearby field by my envious friends and me, the 'practice' was less impressive. We could never seem to get the timing of lighting the wick and releasing the spring on the launch pad properly synchronised. The result was the rocket travelling about twenty yards nearly horizontal to the ground from the action of the launch-pad spring and then nose-diving into the ground before the thrust from the engine came into play. After the nose-dive, repairs to the rocket were generally needed before another attempt to launch could be made. I wish I could claim that eventually we achieved a perfect launch in which the rocket soared skyward and then returned gently to Earth underneath its parachute. Sadly, we never did achieve such a flight and the rocket was eventually consigned to a box of discarded toys. I suspect that few, if any, young boys (sexist but accurate) given this rocket as a present ever got it to perform as advertised, and I think it was probably abandoned by whoever was responsible for its marketing. I certainly do not remember ever seeing it again in any toy shop or department store visited around Christmas time and a recent search on Google has not thrown anymore light on who made this rocket.

The Interview

Before starting RCTS, I had to visit the school to attend an interview with the Headmaster, Mr Church. So along with my mum and dad, off we went to Romford for my first view of the school. I was not impressed. It looked rundown, and when we met him, so did Mr Church. I remember only two things about the interview. The first was that Mr Church asked my parents what religion they were. Mum answered, (my dad always had little to say), 'C of E' (Church of England). I found this surprising as nobody in my family went to church except perhaps for funerals and possibly marriages. Later I realised that at the time, 'C of E' was a catch-all term used by the working class when asked about their religion, even when they were really agnostics or atheists, two terms I presume were not familiar to most working-class people like my parents to describe non-believers.

The second thing I remember about the interview was that the Headmaster asked me what the difference was between an optimist and a pessimist. I was far too nervous to produce anything other than a feeble 'Don't know, sir', so Mr Church was able to produce the punch line, 'A pessimist wears a belt and braces, an optimist wears neither.' My parents and I probably laughed out of politeness although I (and they) only discovered what was funny later.

The New School

The prospect of starting a new school was not one I viewed with eager anticipation. I was a very nervous 11-year-old who had little experience of the world outside my family and friends in Broomwood Gardens. Even travelling to and from RCTS would mean taking two buses which made me apprehensive. But I soon discovered on my first day at the new school that the journey to school and back would be the least of my worries. On my first day, along with other new boys coming through the school gates, to be greeted by groups of older boys shouting abuse at us and referring to us all as 'fags', was not a reassuring start. For me at least, it was downright terrifying.

During the first few days at my new school, it became clear to me that the senior boys of about 15–16 years of age were out of control and most were downright thugs. First year boys like myself were in danger of being the subject of some horrible punishment for 'misdemeanours' such as staring at one of the thugs or not getting out of their way in a corridor. The worst of these punishments was to have your head pushed down the 'bog' (one of the rather unsavoury lavatories). First year boys soon learnt that reporting such punishments to a teacher was not a good idea as it was likely to result in no action by the teacher but increased punishment by the thugs. Most of the staff were probably as scared of the thugs as I was.

I learnt later that in the year I started at RCTS there was no sixth form and no pupils who went to university. Most pupils left at 16 for a career in crime or perhaps as an apprentice to a local plumber. Mr Church had apparently lost interest in improving the school as he was in his last year as Headmaster.

Mr W

RCTS was a co-educational school. As a first year, I was allocated to a class along with a boy from my junior school, Keith, whom I knew, but he was not really a friend. Our form teacher was a Mr Wilson who was French and whose English was often limited. He was very scary, and my first contact with him was when each member of the class had to go individually to his desk at the front of the room to give him details of date of birth, home address etc. As I went to see Mr Wilson, I was probably shaking, if not visibly, certainly inside. Giving my date of birth was no problem, but my address caused an upset. The problem was the spelling of 'Broomwood' which I explained to Mr Wilson when asked was spelt b, r, double o, m, double o, d. It was the double o that was the problem. Mr Wilson repeated the spelling of the word: b, r 'w' m, 'w', d. My efforts to correct him fell on rather stony and short-tempered ground, and Mr Wilson became more and more irate, much to my increasing discomfort and no doubt much to the amusement of the rest of the boys and girls in the class. Eventually, I wrote down the address and I was then sent back to my desk by an obviously very angry Mr Wilson. (It came as no surprise to me that forty years later I heard that Mr Wilson had been charged and found guilty of the murder of his wife. Perhaps her use of 'double o' had sent him over the edge?)

School Lunch

At my primary school, I had generally returned to my house for lunch as this involved only a five-minute walk. At RCTS, of course, I had to take lunch at school. I was a very 'picky' eater with limited experience of anything but sausage and mash, baked beans on toast and sugar sandwiches, the latter being my old mum's speciality.

School lunch came as a great shock: 'fatty' meat lying in congealed gravy, usually cold or at best tepid, bits of chicken in a very thick sauce of doubtful origin and lumpy custard covering some unknown type of pudding. Every lunch time was agony for me.

PT

PT lessons were another contribution to my growing hatred of the school. I was very thin and was embarrassed when changing into my kit in front of the other boys. My embarrassment was not helped by the sadist PT teacher, Mr Cooper, clearly recruited for his hatred of thin, shy boys such as myself. My perception was that he was always picking on me and making some unkind comment about how thin I was.

The very first PT lesson we had also led to a situation that undermined the limited confidence I might have started with. Part of our school uniform was a tie which, when I dressed each day, was tied for me by my mum or one of my sisters. I could not put the tie on myself. Getting dressed in a hurry at the end of the first PT lesson and rushing to get to the next lesson, a French lesson with Mr Wilson, I left my tie off. Back in the classroom, I was the sole pupil not wearing the school tie, offering a perfect opportunity for Mr Wilson to shout at me, particularly as I had no idea how to put the tie in place. Fortunately, Keith came to my rescue and helped me put the tie on, although by the time it was in place the whole class was giggling at my expense with Mr Wilson happy to join in. Sadly, the ground failed to open up to rescue me from the unhappy situation I found myself having to deal with. That weekend, I persuaded one of my sisters to show me how to knot my tie properly and after much practice managed to master the task; on less thing to worry about at school.

Swimming

Even more distressing than the PT lessons was swimming. We had to walk to Romford swimming baths for the lessons. The baths were probably built in the 1930s, and the changing facilities were simply little curtained-off cubicles around the pool. After changing, non-swimmers like myself were given a float and told to get into the shallow end of the pool. The water in the pool was, of course, unheated and being instructed to get one's shoulders under the water was torture. The instructor told us what to do from the relative comfort of the poolside. We then had to walk across the pool holding our float in front of us.

After about thirty minutes when most of us had turned blue with the cold, we had to get dressed very quickly so as to get back to school for whatever lesson was next on the timetable.

I never learned to swim at RCTS; I think the lessons stopped in my second year. Oddly enough, my three youngest sisters could all swim by the time they were in their early teens. They learnt by simply going to Brentwood swimming baths with their friends, nothing to do with lessons at their school. I did try this route, but it was just as bad as the lessons at school. The water was cold, and I was surrounded by noisy children and adults, all of whom could swim, and even some who could jump off the top board some ten or so feet high. I have to say that my Essex Girl sisters were not supportive of my efforts. I think they were embarrassed to have such a wimp of a brother with them.

It is then no wonder that I never learned to swim until I was 25. The adult class I attended was held in a nice warm pool with a very understanding and kind instructor. I took only ten weeks to become a swimmer and to put behind me the torture of earlier attempts to take to the water.

Playing Truant

By the second week of my time at RCTS, I was almost always in tears when walking to catch the first bus for my trip to hell after making protestations to Mum that I was too ill to go to school because of my headache, stomach ache, etc. So, I decided I had to use a different strategy to avoid school as much as possible. This strategy involved taking the first bus into Brentwood but not the second bus into Romford. I then went to Brentwood library for an hour or two, this being a refuge which the rest of my family never entered. After this, I would walk back to my house by a roundabout route getting there at about 4 pm and inform my mother that we had been sent home early because of: (1) dense fog in Romford with the danger of no buses being able to get through to Brentwood, (2) Mr Wilson thought I was unwell, (3) an injury to my knee, ankle, arm or leg and the school nurse thought I should not remain at school. I may have used other even less believable situations to mislead my poor old mum, but she accepted whatever lie I used on a particular day. I used this strategy once or at most twice in a week, which allowed me to at least cope with my fear and loathing of RCTS. After each day of playing truant, I had, of course, to provide Mr W with a letter from my mother of the type, 'Dear Mr Wilson, I am afraid Brian was unwell yesterday with a tummy ache. Yours sincerely, Mrs L. Everitt.' I disguised these notes so the handwriting was not recognisable as my own, although they may have been a little different from each other. Nevertheless, the disguise seemed to achieve its purpose.

No More Truancy and Sandwiches for Lunch

As the weeks of the first term drifted on, I was intelligent enough to know that my truancy could not carry on indefinitely. Fortunately, things at the school got better, and I made some friends. Having friends who could share endless discussions about the latest *Goon Show* or *Hancock's Half Hour* helped a lot. And being able to give a passable impersonation of 'Blue-Bottle' was my trump card.

The problem of the terrible lunches was dealt with by asking my mum if she could ask the school if I could take sandwiches; some of my new friends already did this. This she did and the school agreed. I was then sent off to school each day with my cheese and pickle sandwiches which was a huge relief.

It was amusing that the school frowned on 'sandwich boys' with the dire punishment that such boys were made to eat their lunch in the girls' dinner hall. None of us made any fuss about being treated so badly! (Sadly, I cannot report that 'sandwich girls' were made to eat in the boys' dinner hall, an example of the sexist behaviour prevalent in the 1950s.)

Mr Mitchell

The later months of my first year at RCTS passed without the unhappiness that I had suffered in the first few weeks. And luckily for me and the other first years, our second year started under a new Headmaster, Mr H.G. Mitchell, soon known as 'Mercury Mitchell' amongst the more enlightened pupils. The new head had ideas for turning the school around and improving the academic standards. Over the next few years, a thriving sixth form appeared and fewer people left at the age of 16. Many sixth formers went on to university. 'Mercury Mitchell' and I never really hit it off, but I owe him a lot for opening up wider educational possibilities that none of my sisters had ever enjoyed. Mr Mitchell was probably the main reason that I did not end up aged 17 driving a Ford Anglia with 'Brian' and 'Tracey' across the windscreen and our two children (at least two!) in the back.

Chapter 7

A Death That Ended My Childhood

Discovery

One Saturday, I arrived home from seeing some of my friends and went down the side of the house to the door which led into the kitchen. This was always unlocked when anybody was in the house. I pushed the door, but it would only open a couple of inches. A curtain at the window in the door prevented me from seeing into the kitchen to find out what was blocking the door. I tried two or three more hefty attempts to get the door to move, but whatever was stopping it opening was pretty solid and not to be moved. I went around to the kitchen window at the back of the house and stood on the brick step that surrounded the water outlet so I could see into the kitchen. What was stopping the door opening was my dad lying on the floor. Dad was not a drinker, and even in Essex, lying on the kitchen floor in the middle of the afternoon was not normal.

Clearly, something was wrong. There seemed to be nobody else in the house, as I thought they would have heard the noise I had been making, so I ran to get my eldest sister Joan who lived a couple of hundred yards away. Fortunately, she was in, and after explaining what I had seen, we both raced back to Broomwood Gardens.

Joan thought Mum might be in having an afternoon nap in the bedroom. Joan was correct, and after knocking on the front door several times, Mum appeared to ask what all the knocking was about. After a few words of explanation, we all walked the few steps along the hall to the kitchen to be confronted by my dear old dad lying there. Mum and I burst into tears because the body appeared to us to be lifeless. Eldest sister Joan was made of sterner stuff and checked to see if my dad was breathing which, amazingly, he was. Having no phone in the house, Joan went to the closest telephone box and rang 999 for an ambulance. My dad was rushed to the nearest hospital. Mum went with him in the ambulance, and I stayed with Joan.

Waiting

Soon after the ambulance had left, Joan and I walked the short distance to where my sister Pat lived and told her the news about Dad. She was very upset and thought she should go to the hospital. By this time, Joan also wanted to find out what was happening, so I was dumped on Roberts's parents who very kindly agreed to look after me until Mum and the others returned from the hospital.

Somehow all my other sisters heard the news about Dad, and they all went to the hospital to see him. About 9 pm everybody returned from the hospital to Broomwood Gardens, and I was collected from Roberts's house. My sisters were all in a terrible state, and it wasn't difficult to work out that the news about Dad was not good. Mum took control and made everybody something to eat and handed out lots of cups of tea. I think in her heart, she knew Dad was not going to last much longer. Eventually, the sisters returned to their various homes, except for Joan who decided she should stay with Mum and me. I was sent to bed rather tearful and aware that it was very likely that my dad was going to die soon.

The next day, everybody except me returned to the hospital, and this time I was left in the care of some of my brothers-in-law. They tried to keep me from becoming too sad by playing cards or anything else I suggested. Soon, a few of my sisters arrived back very upset because Dad was now unconscious. It was clearly only a matter of time, and at about four o'clock in the afternoon, Mum and Joan arrived back from the hospital to tell us all that Dad had died. He was 61.

Funeral

The next few days were difficult for everybody particularly, of course, for Mum. Clearly Dad had no large pot of money to leave her, and she must have been very worried about how she would cope. But she dealt with this and with her grief over Dad not being around anymore very bravely. I was looked after by my sisters and brothers-in-law, and one day my sister Connie and her husband Dell took me off to watch cricket at the Gallows Corner ground near Romford. Essex was playing, but I cannot remember their opponents. However, I do remember that when we were walking around the ground, we spotted Trevor Bailey chatting to some friends, perhaps explaining to them why he wasn't playing in this match.

Dad's funeral took place about 10 days after he died. Mum did not want me to go to the funeral; perhaps she thought I would be very upset. Anyway, off I went again to spend the day with Robert's parents. On reflection, I think I was quite upset about not being allowed to be at the funeral which was held at Bentley Church, with Dad being buried in the grounds of the church.

I was picked up when everybody returned from the funeral and heard a little about it. Although people were still very sad, there was perhaps an acceptance of what had happened and lots of stories about Dad were exchanged. Although there was little overt talk about 'love' in our family, it was clear that Dad was much loved by my sisters and Mum and, of course, by me. Dad was kind and gentle but not given to long speeches. I have always wished I could have asked him about his experiences in the First World War, but I was too young at the time to delve into this. I suspect though that these experiences were what gave Dad his quiet and caring persona.

Child No Longer

In the days that followed the funeral, the house seemed very different without Dad. As my youngest sister Vera had recently married her boyfriend George and moved out of the house, there remained only Mum and I. It was clear that Mum was considering how to get on with her life, and I was perceptive enough to know that everything was now going to be different, and from the financial point of view, even more of a struggle. I was going to have to grow up very quickly and help Mum with the problems that she was very likely to have to face. I was 12 years old, and there would be no more childhood memories of playing in the street or roaming over Weald Park. My 'childhood' had come to an end.

Epilogue

A very brief account of some of what happened to me after my childhood ended.

After Dad died, Mum and I had to settle into a new lifestyle. I was now the only one of her children still living at home and she had only a widows' pension to live on. The first decision we had to make involved the pigeons and the pigeon loft. I had neither the time, what with the increasing demands of school, or the inclination to continue the pigeon racing, so both the pigeons and the loft had to go. Some of Dad's friends at the club rallied around and bought our pigeons and dismantled the loft. It was sad to see Dad's source of so much pleasure disappear.

Once the pigeon loft had gone, I took over responsibility for making the garden look respectable. This took a lot of my time at weekends and combined with homework meant that time spent with my friends was minimal. Sadly, my trips to the cinema with Mum also stopped; she lost interest in going out to watch films and preferred spending time in the evenings watching the television we now had. I was drawn in to watch with her, even doing my homework on the living room table, whilst taking in the subtleties of *Coronation Street* and

Emergency Ward Ten. My evening would end at about 10 pm, and I would slip off to my bed which was now in Mum and Dad's old bedroom with Mum taking over the other reasonably sized room which had once housed three or more of my sisters. The occasional lodger that my mum took in to help her finances slept in the wardrobe-sized room.

One summer when I was 13, Mum found enough money to take me on holiday to Butlin's Holiday Camp in Clacton. These camps were founded by Billy Butlin to provide affordable holidays for ordinary British families. Not sure that Mum and I qualified as 'ordinary'. I was still quite shy, and being shy meant that I found the atmosphere at the camp unappealing to say the least. Jolly Redcoats trying to get people to join in each day's activities wasn't really my cup of tea. And as I couldn't swim, activities in the pool were also not for me. We never went to Butlin's again, which was fine by me.

Mum and I did go on holidays with my sister Iris and her husband Stan. Generally, a couple of my growing number of nieces and nephews came with us, most often to sunny Jaywick. We all stayed in a large house very close to the beach with the address, 3 Sea Pink Way. Jaywick is now considered to be the most deprived town in the UK, but I looked forward to our holidays there. I suppose I was very easily pleased and had no experience of staying anywhere that might these days be considered more wonderful than Jaywick (which is probably almost anywhere).

Although there was not a great deal of playing in the streets now, my interest in science that took root when I was about six or seven provided some alternative recreations. I had grown particularly fond of chemistry and astronomy.

Eventually, interest in chemistry led to my exploration of how to make explosions and explosives. Making explosives proved remarkably easy once I found that the gas driving the gas cooker in the kitchen was coal gas and contained hydrogen. I knew that under certain circumstances hydrogen and oxygen could be made to combine violently to produce water. So, I employed a syrup tin with a hole punched in the bottom and in the lid and filled the tin with gas by simply placing the hole in the bottom over the gas supply once one of the gas rings of the cooker had been removed. The tin was then placed on two pieces of wood so that there was a gap between the bottom of the tin and the ground. The hole at the top of the tin was then lit. After a short time, there would be a small explosion and the lid of the tin would blow off. Hydrogen in the coal gas had combined with oxygen in the air to form water with an associated mildly explosive reaction.

But my real goal was to produce a more powerful explosion from materials that I could readily get my hands on. And luckily, I happened to read in a gardening article in the paper about the weed killer, sodium chlorate, a chemical that the article stressed was inert until mixed but warned that it could become dangerously explosive when mixed with any combustible material and subjected to heat. By visiting a garden supplies shop in Brentwood, I found it was possible to buy a large tin of sodium chlorate relatively cheaply and without any awkward questions from the shop assistant, so I did. After a number of experiments which fortunately I survived, I found that a successful 'bomb' could be made by mixing a quantity of the weed killer with a similar quantity of sugar and pack it into a tin with a small hole in which you could insert a piece of jetex wick. I would then take the tin to the bottom of the garden, cover it with earth but leaving the wick just visible above ground. Then it was light wick and retire quickly to the side of the house. The explosion would send remnants of the tin in all directions including towards the house and once or twice hitting the windows. This caused Mum to worry about my safety and on reflection I thought she was correct; consequently, I abandoned plans to make bigger explosions using sulphur instead of sugar mixed with the sodium chlorate. That I am still here today suggests this was a wise decision. (It is interesting to note that sodium chlorate was banned across Europe in 2009.)

The second science-based hobby I took up was astronomy. When I was 14, I spent about £12 on a three-inch refracting telescope and a six-foot tripod stand. The telescope was perfect for observing the Moon, and I would make drawings of the surface of the Moon. I could also just about make out the rings of Saturn, and the telescope made it possible to see some star clusters, and once or twice I think the 'smudge' of light I observed was the Andromeda galaxy, two million light years away. My astronomical adventures were first interrupted by a growing interest in girls and then finished completely for the same reason, when I sold the telescope and stand for a bargain price of £10 when I was about 17. I am afraid this time it was definitely sex trumping curiosity. But Mum and Dad's present of *The Junior Science Encyclopaedia* when I was eight had not been entirely wasted.

So, the years passed by with me doing well at school academically, getting colours for cricket and athletics (all that sports activity in Broomwood Gardens had clearly not been a waste of time), and being made school chess captain. From school, I went to University in London so that I could live at home with Mum.

After graduating I worked for a short time for the Civil Service and then moved into a university career. Eventually I became a statistician in a research Institute of the University of London. The place was full of very clever people much cleverer than me and much more informed about almost any subject one might mention except, luckily for me, statistics, although in all honesty there were a good proportion of people who probably knew far more than I did even about that topic. But the Institute was an interesting place to work and I quickly grew to like the being there and made friends with quite a few people. Although I was never a brilliant academic statistician, I did find I had a talent for writing readable books on statistical topics and eventually I wrote over 70 such books. I was made Professor in 1987 (almost certainly undeserved but coming from Essex I had learnt early in life never to look a gift-horse in the mouth).

My first marriage failed, and we eventually divorced. One good thing that arose from the marriage was my lovely daughter, Joanna, whom I managed to remain close to even after the marriage broke up. Many, many affairs followed, some lasting a few days but one that lasted several years; this one was with a special woman who in the end I treated very, very badly. I imagine that she has never really forgiven me. Eventually, I met a lovely calm, younger woman; she was 27 and I was 43. A few years later, we had a daughter, Rachel, who was just as wonderful as Joanna! Just before Rachel was four years old, we married. I was then 52.

I retired when I was 60, I am writing this book during my 75th year.

Sisters

My sisters all married and all but one, had children. I think many of their marriages were difficult, but their childhoods had made them resilient enough to not always dwell on their own problems, and they were all, without exception, kind and considerate to other people. The three older sisters died in the order they were born, Joan in her 60s, Iris in her late 50s and Hilda also in her late 50s. The first of the three younger sisters to die was Vera, when she was in her 70s, followed soon by Connie also in her late 70s. My last sister to die was Pat when she was 83 which was somewhat surprising because she had the most difficult marriage and life of all my sisters. But in her later years, she was always a delight to visit and always very funny. Her stories were sometimes 'economical with the truth' but never dull. I miss her greatly.

Mum and Dad – Final Memories

What do I remember most about my parents? Well, my mum was nearly always busy; there was no washing machine to deal with the large piles of dirty clothes mostly generated by my sisters. Mum was constantly employed pushing clothes around in a large gas heated copper; rinsing and mangling followed. The mangle was hand turned, and Mum certainly had the arms to deal with it, probably built up by years of hard physical work. And some mornings, she would go out to clean the houses of various people. Sometimes, Mum took me along, and I do remember thinking how large these houses were and assuming the owners were very rich, which of course they were compared to us. Most of all though, I remember that they gave Mum and me cheese rolls for lunch which were so good!

Mum was almost always the person who had to deal with my sisters and with me if we had misbehaved. We could, however, always judge the level of any misdemeanour we were charged with because if it was Dad who gave us a ticking off, it was high on the bad behaviour scale. I cannot remember much physical punishment being meted out by either parent. Perhaps, one of my sisters would be smacked by Mum when she was completely in despair about something that had happened.

Amongst all the difficult times there must have been, Mum kept her sense of fun although, at times, her idea of fun was not the same of some of the victims of her little escapades. For example, one such escapade involved spiders. My sister Pat was terrified of spiders of any size, but in particular, she hated the monster specimens that lived in the hayfield at the back of the house before the school was built there. Mum had no fear of spiders and would sometimes find a large one in the bathroom when Pat and my other sisters were perhaps in the sitting room listening to the radio. She would then slip quietly into the room holding the spider in a clenched fist which she would then open right under Pat's nose. Pat's screams nearly brought the house down. The rest of us couldn't stop laughing, which was not very kind really.

In retrospect, I like to think of Mum's apparently cruel joke as an early use of the psychological treatment called flooding to help people with spider phobias.

Mum died when she was 78 having by that time many grandchildren who loved their gran greatly. She was buried in the same grave as Dad in Bentley Church. We had a family collection and bought a gravestone to mark their grave. I still go to visit the grave but not as often as I should.

Mum had had a tough life but managed most of the time to see the funny side of things. She was of a time when deep analysis of one's life was only for those who were rich enough to have the time for such an indulgence. For Mum, her life was simply what it was, and she just had to get on with all the ups and the many downs that came along.

Dad was always in the background of my childhood. He took a backseat in almost all the happenings in our house. I never remember him shouting at any of us and never at my mum. He was happiest just sitting in his chair by the side of the fire continuously smoking his roll-up cigarettes and reading the paper. He hardly ever removed his flat hat, and I can still remember the smell of his hat, acquired mostly from his heavy smoking. Under the hat, my dad had a full head of white hair. I have been forever grateful for inheriting Dad's hair genes. I would often sit on his lap, and we would share a few words about the pigeons or about the sports news in the paper. I regret I was never old enough to ask him about his experiences in the First World War or about his own childhood before he died.

I presume my parents loved their children and each other, but I don't think I ever heard either of them voicing this love directly to any of their daughters, their son or to each other. In the 1950s, I suspect, this was not unusual amongst working class with large families trying to get through life with limited income. But if the word love is never spoken, does it mean there isn't any love? I don't think so.

I can't say this lack of an overt display of affection from my parents worried me too much. I was far too interested in my library books, my comics and my friends to even give the matter more than the briefest of consideration. As long as one or other of my parents was around to hug me during a thunderstorm, of which I was terrified, that was fine and was proof enough for me as to how much they cared for their son.

The memory of my childhood that is most important for me is the freedom I was allowed. My parents never forced any religious or political views on me. And my friends and I could play in the street or wander over to Weald Park to fish for newts completely unsupervised by any adult. There were no mobile phones for my friends and me in the 1950s, no Xboxes, no laptops and no travel to exotic places that we had probably never heard of. But in the place of these childhood experiences available in the twenty-first century, my friends and I invented things to do and games to play so that we could simply have fun in each other's company. That old saying, 'We have no money so we will have to think,' comes to mind once again. And the trips I took with my parents were always special, perhaps because they were relatively few and far between. Will children of today reflect on their trips to the USA, China and other far-flung places with as much pleasure as I remember my trips to Southend and Clacton? I have my doubts.

Index